❧ THE ❧
HEALTHY TABLE

LUIZ RATTO
WITH ANN VOLKWEIN

❧ THE ❧

HEALTHY TABLE

SIMPLE, DELICIOUS HOME COOKING

ReganBooks
An Imprint of HarperCollins Publishers

HarperCollins books may be purchased for educational, business, or sales promotional use. For information please write: Special Markets Department, HarperCollins Publishers Inc., 10 East 53rd Street, New York, NY 10022.

FIRST EDITION

Designed by Dan Taylor

Printed on acid-free paper

Library of Congress Cataloging-in-Publication Data

Ratto, Luiz.
    The healthy table : simple, delicious home cooking / Luiz Ratto with Ann Volkwein.—1st ed.
       p. cm.
    Includes index.
    ISBN 0-06-008867-2
    1. Cookery. 2. Reducing diets—Recipes. I. Volkwein, Ann. II. Title.

TX714 .R38 2003
641.5—dc21

2002031859

03   04   05   06   07   WB/RRD   10 9 8 7 6 5 4 3 2 1

To cooks everywhere

Contents

Introduction	x
Cooking Tips	3
Techniques	4
Ingredients	5
Equipment	8
Appetizers	10
Soups	28
Salads and Grains	47
Vegetables	67
Fish, Shellfish, and Poultry	97
Weekend Recipes	124
Desserts	146
Basic Recipes	160
Acknowledgments	172
Index	175

INTRODUCTION

What if I told you that if you slightly change your eating habits you could add many—and healthier—years to your life? Maybe you would agree with me, but would you really be willing to try it? You may think that this means you have to stop eating any fat or sugars, start eating tofu or tempeh, or even follow one of those horrible diets that don't allow you to have any pleasure at the table. The good news is that you don't have to make drastic changes. You can start slowly, step by step, knowing that if you keep it simple you won't notice any difference.

Although I have been a personal chef for ten years, I see myself more as a home cook rather than a traditional professional chef. I don't have intensive classic training in schools and apprenticeships. I've learned from occasional courses about designing balanced menus, the timing of recipes, and nutritional values of ingredients, but my recipes have remained uncomplicated. As a personal chef I don't have the fast-paced pressures of the restaurant kitchen, but I also don't have a kitchen staff doing all my prep work. What I do have is the great advantage of bringing my food directly to the dining room, where I get instant feedback. This book is a reflection of my experience: healthy recipes that you can confidently reproduce in your home kitchens and bring to your own tables full of family and friends.

Home cooking *can* be healthy. The comforting, flavor-filled qualities of a home-cooked meal can also be a good source of nutrients and vitamins that you need to sustain yourself and your family in good health. I have developed a style of cooking that satisfies and impresses without being overly rich or complex. My recipes emphasize the use of fresh ingredients and whole grains, and a minimum of processed or canned products and red meat, while never compromising on flavor. Above all, keep it simple.

How do you incorporate this food philosophy into your life? Well, let's start from the beginning. In my opinion, your knowledge of cooking comes from three different sources: your heritage, personal taste and the tastes of the people you cook for, and techniques you learn through study. First, from your family you learn the traditional dishes that go back generations. Every ethnicity has its particular style and use of ingredients that are common and familiar. Sit down and make a list of your family recipes, how your grandma used to cook and what dishes your wife, husband, kids, or friends enjoy. Then make a list of the meals and ingredients you like best. Start to analyze all the ingredients and the way you use them in recipes. Begin by making small changes. See if you can use a little less fat, more vegetables, fewer processed or canned products, and more fiber and nutrients. As I've said, keep it simple. For example, in your favorite salad, are you using a fat-loaded Caesar or blue cheese dressing? Maybe you aren't aware that it's possible to make equally creamy dressings without using cheese or even oil. My Cooking Tips section provides advice on how to substitute as well as hints about ingredients and how to improvise.

I am originally from Brazil, a country where cooking is based mainly on fresh ingredients and most meals have at least two or three different vegetable dishes. That's my heritage and it's a huge influence on my cooking style. Brazilian cooking is a reflection of the land's richness. The tropical weather and unlimited natural resources bring an abundance of flavors to the table. The different cultures and ethnicities that form Brazil's population also enrich the exotic tastes found in Brazilian cookery. The country was colonized by the Portuguese, who contributed ingredients like olive oil, onions, garlic, parsley, and scallions to the cuisine. Other influences include the native Indians, who use banana, papaya, pineapple, root vegetables, and squashes, and West Africans who brought the taste for okra, rice, collard greens, pumpkin, and spices. The result is a cuisine that appeals to all the senses, rich in taste but also very, very rich in vitamins and nutrients. Nonetheless, while my recipes are influenced by my heritage, they are by no means strictly Brazilian. For example, after getting a list of his favorite foods, I developed dishes that follow the taste and preferences of my boss, Mr. Michael Fuchs, and the sophisticated palates of his guests. His insistence on health-minded cooking has been an exciting challenge, and many of my recipes are the tasty fruits of our collaboration.

You'll see I have a chapter for Weekend Recipes. These recipes are more elaborate, designed for when you have more time for entertaining—and you'll notice they're sometimes a little less healthy, but that's okay on occasion! Remember, if you adjust your cooking as I have described, it's not about counting calories. It's about generally eating well, taking an approach that isn't extreme, with a commitment to fresh ingredients. Food is a labor of love and love is an ingredient that has to be present in every meal you put together; it makes the food taste better. So, use your imagination, put a little music on, ask your kids to help you, or invite your partner to a midnight cooking session. There is nothing better than having your loved ones with you when you are in the kitchen—after all, you are cooking for them too.

COOKING TIPS

Before I offer my cooking tips, I want to assure you that my cooking style is uncomplicated and doesn't require a vast knowledge of technique to replicate. However, as chef in charge, you will be left with some decisions and choices. The recipes are easy to follow and they allow for modifications and substitutions. Don't be afraid to try them; let yourself have fun in the kitchen. You already know the taste of the individual ingredients you're using. How they will taste in different combinations, prepared using different methods, will vary depending on your sense of adventure. I'm talking common sense here—just don't mix strawberries and black beans; most likely it won't work.

One of the things I consider fundamental to my cooking is the use of high-quality, fresh ingredients. Examine vegetables, fruits, and herbs for freshness. Check the meats and fish for smell and appearance. Give preference to local products for freshness and to organic produce and meat, as they are free of pesticides and often have better flavor and more nutrients. Nowadays you can find almost everything you need in health food stores or local supermarkets.

TECHNIQUES

KNIFE TECHNIQUE Slicing, chopping, or mincing an ingredient alters the taste of the final dish. The manner in which you cut an ingredient, combined with the time you cook it, can intensify the flavor or make the flavor blend with other ingredients. Smaller cuts spread the taste of the ingredient throughout the dish, while larger cuts preserve the flavor of the individual ingredient.

SAUTÉING I like to use large nonstick skillets (unless I am deglazing, see below) because I can get away with using a lot less oil. I sauté in a large number of recipes in this book and give instructions for temperatures and cooking times. Be aware, however, that as your stovetop and pans will differ from the ones I use, you have to exercise your judgment and be more watchful initially when adhering to the cooking times and heat levels.

TO COVER OR NOT TO COVER? If you want to reduce the amount of a sauce or the liquid content in a dish, don't use the cover. But if your aim is to keep the liquid, then use the cover—this also facilitates faster cooking time for certain dishes, as the food steams in the liquid (as in a stew, for example). When you roast a turkey or a chicken, cover the bird with aluminum foil for the first third of the roasting time. This process keeps the meat juicy while the cooking process continues.

CARAMELIZING Some vegetables have a high sugar content. As you cook them and the sugars start to come out, they can become brown. This process is called caramelization, and is often used with onions. Just be aware that the browner they become, the more sugars are being cooked off, and the more bitter the ultimate taste.

DEGLAZING This process is great for starting soups and sauces to enhance their flavors and colors. Sauté the ingredients until they start to stick to the bottom of the pan (be careful not to burn them). Then add liquid (water, wine, rum, or whatever you prefer) to the pan and stir to "clean" the bottom of the pan and incorporate the caramelized bits into the ingredients you're cooking.

REDUCING SAUCES OR STOCKS This is a great method to use to intensify or give more pungency to the taste. In many cases it also thickens the consistency of the dish you're preparing. Simply boil or simmer (slow boil) the sauce or stock to reduce it.

INGREDIENTS

SALT AND PEPPER Salt and pepper added at the end of the cooking process give you a better sense of the seasoning you want to add to the food. If you add them early, the flavors of salt and pepper will intensify as some of the liquid boils away and you will have less control of the outcome. Remember that if you use too little, you can always add more later. Also keep in mind that salt makes ingredients release water and/or shrink, so salt should be added early only when this effect is desired.

HERBS *Fresh* herbs are a must in any kind of cooking. They give food an incomparable taste, help avoid the use of too much fat (butter and oils), and at the same time make the final dish visually appealing. Personal taste dictates the use of an herb, but some combinations are known to work well:

> Basil—tomato sauce, pesto sauce
> Cilantro—fish, salads
> Dill—yogurt, cucumbers, salmon
> Oregano—tomato sauce
> Rosemary—chicken, lamb, potatoes
> Parsley—almost everything
> Sage—turkey
> Thyme—soups, vegetables

BEANS Every time you use beans you will have to decide whether or not to use the canned product. My opinion is simple: Fresh beans taste better. They are not preserved in brines that are high in sodium and other chemicals that alter their flavor completely. On the other hand, cooking beans from scratch is time consuming, so use fresh beans as frequently as time allows. Sort them carefully, wash them, and soak them overnight. As you cook them, skim off the foam that accumulates in the pan. Add salt at the end of the cooking process, because beans will shrink and get tough if you add salt too early.

GRAINS Start by placing the grain in a dry saucepan and "toasting" it for a minute or two over high heat, always stirring with a wooden spoon. Toasting releases some of the flavor of the grain and speeds up the cooking time. After toasting, add hot water, which in most cases is twice the amount of the grain you're using. As the grain starts to boil, cover the pan, reduce the heat to the lowest setting on your stovetop, and cook for the desired time. Times vary according to the type of grain you're using and the softness desired. The best method is to check the pan periodically while cooking. If the grains aren't soft enough, just add a little more water and cook a little longer. Then transfer to a colander or a strainer and let it rest while you prepare the vegetable sauté you'd like to add. This technique allows you to infuse more flavors into the grains. Instead of mushy or discolored ingredients, you're serving a vibrant, flavorful dish.

white rice, quinoa, millet	15 minutes
barley, brown rice	25 to 35 minutes
rye, wild rice, spelt	35 to 45 minutes

NUTS Nuts such as almonds, cashews, pistachios, walnuts, pecans, pine nuts, and hazelnuts add another dimension of flavor and texture to salads, desserts, and more. Try not to overdo them, because they all have very high fat content, although it is the healthier unsaturated fat.

SEEDS As with nuts, seeds can be used on numerous dishes. They increase the percentage of fiber and lend a lot of taste. Pumpkin, poppy, sesame, and flax seeds are my favorite varieties.

DRIED FRUITS Raisins (yellow and black), cherries, cranberries, blueberries, and currants also diversify textures and flavors and add a contrasting sweetness to savory dishes.

ROASTED PEPPERS There are three ways to roast peppers: on the grill, under the broiler, or on a gas stovetop with direct heat. Brush some oil on the skin of the peppers and bring them to the heat source. Keep turning the peppers as the skin burns and gets black, then put them in a paper bag for 5 minutes to help steam the skin off. Finally, wash off the skin under cold running water.

GRILLED VEGETABLES Grilled vegetables are great to serve on salads, with barbecued meats, or even as the main component of a summer dinner (see the recipe for Rolled Eggplant on page 142). Try different vegetables and marinades, rubbing spices or herbs, sauces or oils. The sky's the limit here in terms of imagination. Here are some suggestions:

GRILLABLE VEGETABLES: eggplant, zucchini, sweet or hot peppers, carrots, asparagus, mushrooms, green beans, fennel, onions, corn on the cob, and so on

RUBBING SPICES: cardamom, paprika, cumin, nutmeg, Cajun spices, black or white pepper

FOR MARINADES

HERBS AND SEASONINGS: oregano, thyme, rosemary, parsley, cilantro, sage, tarragon, and basil; minced onions; garlic; scallions; and ginger

SAUCES: soy, teriyaki, oyster, mirin, tamari, hoisin

VINEGARS: balsamic, white, apple cider, rice, red wine

OILS: olive, sesame, canola, sunflower, safflower, corn

SALAD DRESSINGS I don't use any oil in my salad dressings; it's a good way of cutting down the amount of fat in a meal. Instead of oil use puréed fruits; they will break down the acidity from the vinegars and even emulsify and give body to the dressing. On the chart below you'll see four columns starting with four different fruits. The ingredients in each column are interchangeable, giving you many options for dressings.

1 cup blueberries	1 cup cherries	1 cup pineapple	1 cup papaya
1 garlic clove, minced	1 medium Vidalia onion, minced	1 tablespoon, ginger minced	¼ red onion, minced
2 tablespoons minced parsley	3 scallion stalks, green part only, minced	2 tablespoons minced cilantro	4 basil leaves, minced
¾ cup balsamic vinegar	½ cup red wine vinegar	½ cup lime juice	½ cup white vinegar
Salt and pepper to taste			

"FISH IN A BAG" Parchment paper, aluminum foil, a paper bag brushed with oil, or even banana leaves can be used here. Cut parchment paper in circular shapes about 12 inches in diameter, fold in half, and place the fish on the center of the half circle. Top with a little oil, seasonings, and herbs. Fold the other half of the parchment over the ingredients and crimp the edges to seal, leaving some air around the food. They will steam-cook when baked at 400°F. for 10 to 15 minutes.

LEFTOVERS A very important component in home cooking is leftovers. As we all know, some foods taste better the next day. Improvisation plays a big role here. You can modify some leftovers by adding new ingredients or simply reusing them in a different way. For example, take the recipe for Brown Rice with Cashew Nuts and Cranberries (page 63). Let's say you have 1½ cups left over from last night's dinner. Add some corn and peas sautéed in garlic and onions, some parsley and beaten egg whites, and you can make brown rice pancakes with the mixture, a whole different dish. To the same brown rice recipe you can add vinegar or salad dressing and serve with a mixed greens salad. Add some steamed vegetables, and you have a completely new dish for lunch. The same idea goes for other leftovers. Grilled vegetables can be transformed into a delicious pasta or soup. Adding a new ingredient like roasted onions or simply a fruit can change salad dressings. You get the idea.

EQUIPMENT

Good equipment makes cooking easier, but as my equipment list illustrates, complex, high-tech gadgetry isn't necessary. A lot of what I have listed here you will already have in your kitchen. Above all, the most important equipment to have is a good set of knives and a set of stainless steel, nonstick pans. Try to arrange your kitchen so that you have easy access to all your tools while cooking.

KNIVES

3- or 4-inch paring knife

10- or 12-inch chef's knife

8- or 10-inch carving knife

Serrated 8- or 10-inch bread knife

Kitchen scissors

Sharpening steel

Sharpening stone

POTS, PANS, AND BAKING DISHES

2-quart saucepan with lid

3-quart saucepan with lid

5-quart saucepan with lid

Stockpot

2 or 3 sauté pans (skillets), of different sizes

Wok

Steaming pan/basket

2 or 3 baking dishes, various sizes

Six to eight ¼-cup ramekins

Two 8- or 9-inch springform pans

Large roasting pan with rack

MISCELLANEOUS

5 wooden spoons, various sizes

1 or 2 large stainless steel spoons

1 or 2 large stainless steel slotted spoons

Stainless steel whisk

1 or 2 stainless steel ladles

2 pairs of tongs

1 or 2 stainless steel spatulas

1 or 2 rubber spatulas

Set of glass measuring cups (1, 2, and 4 cups)

Set of stainless-steel measuring cups (¼, ⅓, ½, and 1 cup)

Set of measuring spoons (¼, ½, and 1 teaspoon; 1 tablespoon)

Salad spinner

Set of mixing bowls (preferably glass)

Four-sided grater

Vegetable peeler

2 chopping boards (wooden or plastic)

1 pepper mill

2 or 3 strainers of different sizes

Food processor

Blender

Electric mixer

APPETIZERS

Appetizers are like the foreplay before a good meal. I like mine to have visual appeal and be diverse in texture and flavor. Tempt your guests with a refreshing Ceviche, tantalizing Crabmeat-Stuffed Mushrooms, or a spicy Green Grape Salsa.

ANTIPASTO 8 SERVINGS

Traditional Italian antipasto uses a lot of olive oil and tends to be a bit heavy. In my version I use just a little oil and a long, slow baking technique, which allows the vegetables to cook in their natural juices. This is not only a wonderful appetizer, it's great in a sandwich too.

Preheat the oven to 200°F.

Using a casserole with a cover or a deep baking dish that you can cover with aluminum foil, start to build layers with the ingredients, beginning with 8 tomato halves in the bottom, then about 4 slices of the eggplants, followed by some yellow pepper slices, zucchini slices, and a few onion and garlic slices. Cover with a lot of thyme and finish with salt and pepper to taste and 1 tablespoon of olive oil. Start another layer with tomatoes, repeating all the other ingredients, but this time use oregano instead of thyme, and season with salt and pepper and 1 more tablespoon of olive oil. The last layer begins again with tomatoes and the same order of ingredients. Cover with parsley this time, then the 8 remaining tomato halves. Sprinkle on some more salt and pepper and drizzle on the last tablespoon of olive oil. Cover with aluminum foil or a lid and bake for at least 8 hours.

Let cool and refrigerate for 2 hours before serving.

16 plum tomatoes, halved

4 small Japanese eggplants, sliced on the bias ½ inch thick

3 roasted yellow peppers, seeded and sliced ½ inch thick

1 large zucchini, sliced on the bias ¼ inch thick

1 large Vidalia onion, thinly sliced

6 garlic cloves, thinly sliced

2 bunches of thyme (about 40 sprigs)

Salt and pepper

3 tablespoons olive oil

2 bunches of oregano (about 40 sprigs)

2 bunches of parsley (about 2 cups)

CEVICHE 8 SERVINGS

Ceviche is popular in Peru as a cold appetizer. Although prepared in a raw state, the fish is actually "cooked" by the acids in the marinade. There are just three components to this recipe: the fish, the marinade, and the seasonings. You can serve this as an elegant first course or even on a bed of greens as a refreshing summer main dish.

½ pound bay scallops

½ pound calamari

1 pound sea bass or snapper

½ cup fresh lime juice

½ cup fresh lemon juice

¼ cup olive oil

Salt and pepper

2 tablespoons jalapeño or serrano peppers, seeded and minced

1 large red onion, thinly sliced

½ cup coarsely chopped cilantro

Rinse the scallops, calamari, and fish thoroughly, pat them dry, and cut them into bite-sized pieces. Reserve in the refrigerator.

In a bowl, whisk together well the lime and lemon juices and the olive oil. Add the seafood to the bowl and toss gently with the liquid. Add salt and pepper to taste, cover with plastic wrap, and refrigerate for 1 hour.

Add all the remaining ingredients, mix well, and refrigerate, covered, for 1 hour more. Serve chilled.

CRABMEAT-STUFFED MUSHROOMS 8 SERVINGS

Unlike many stuffed mushroom recipes, mine doesn't use bread, cheese, or mayonnaise to bind the stuffing. This isn't necessary because the mushroom cap makes a natural, scooped container for the delicate crabmeat mixture.

In a large saucepan filled with boiling water, boil the mushrooms for 2 minutes. Drain and rinse under cold water.

In a large skillet over high heat, add the olive oil and sauté the garlic for 1 minute. Add the mushrooms and sauté for 1 minute. Add the wine and cook for only 2 minutes. Add parsley and salt to taste and stir well. Reserve.

In a large bowl, add the stuffing ingredients. Mix well. Season to taste with salt.

One by one, stuff the mushrooms with the crabmeat mixture. Serve at room temperature.

MUSHROOMS

24 large white button mushrooms

2 tablespoons olive oil

2 garlic cloves, minced

¼ cup white wine

1 tablespoon minced parsley

Salt

STUFFING

12 ounces big lump crabmeat

1 teaspoon red pepper flakes

1 teaspoon ground mustard

1 tablespoon celery seeds

1 teaspoon ground black pepper

½ small Spanish onion, minced

2 plum tomatoes, seeded and diced

2 tablespoons minced parsley

Salt

GREEN GRAPE SALSA MAKES 4 CUPS

Allow yourself a little extra time for this recipe, as there is a lot of chopping involved. Try to keep a uniform size for all the ingredients (other than the jalapeño) as you dice. The heat of the jalapeño balances the sweetness of the grapes beautifully.

1 large red onion, diced

6 medium plum tomatoes, seeded and diced

1 yellow pepper, seeded and diced

1 jalapeño pepper, minced, with seeds

1 green pepper, seeded and diced

2 cups green grapes, cut into eighths

2 tablespoons red wine vinegar

Juice of 1 lime

½ cup tomato juice (see Note)

½ cup minced cilantro

2 tablespoons minced chives

In a glass bowl, add all the ingredients. Mix well. Cover with plastic wrap and refrigerate for a few hours. Serve the salsa with tortilla chips or as an accompaniment to fish or chicken.

NOTE: If you don't have a juicer, use canned tomato juice, but make the effort to find a good brand and keep in mind that organic is always preferred.

GUACAMOLE 8 SERVINGS

Serve this perennial favorite with blue and white corn tortilla chips and a separate bowl of salsa.

Cut the avocados in half, discard the pits, and scoop the pulp out into a bowl. Using a fork, break down the pulp into the consistency you would like the guacamole to have.

Add all the other ingredients and mix well. Cover and refrigerate or serve immediately.

3 ripe avocados

½ large red onion, chopped

5 plum tomatoes, seeded and diced

2 garlic cloves, minced

1 jalapeño pepper, seeded and minced

1 teaspoon ground cumin

2 tablespoons fresh lime juice

¼ cup chopped cilantro

Salt and pepper

SALMON SPREAD ROLL-UPS 8 SERVINGS

The tartness of the apple, the rich taste of the salmon, and the crunch of the alfalfa sprouts make these sandwiches appealing on many levels. Cut on the bias, they become the perfect party finger food. The variations are endless, but I have suggested a couple of my favorite combinations below.

Preheat the oven to 400°F.

Peel, core, and thinly slice the apples, dipping the sections in lime juice to prevent them from browning.

Place the tortillas on a baking sheet and bake them for 2 minutes to make them just a little bit crispy. (Note that if you bake the tortillas longer than that they will break when you try to roll them.)

Spread the salmon mixture on three quarters of each tortilla, then layer on the green apples, alfalfa sprouts, and chives.

Fold the bare bottom section of the tortilla over the filling and roll upward into a tight cylinder (see illustration).

Cut the rolls on the bias in quarters. To serve, arrange the little spirals on a plate over a bed of greens or alfalfa sprouts

2 large Granny Smith apples

Juice of 1 lime

8 whole wheat tortillas

Salmon Spread (recipe follows)

4 cups alfalfa sprouts

1 cup minced chives

SALMON SPREAD 8 SERVINGS

8 ounces salmon steak

½ cup soft tofu

2 tablespoons minced capers

2 tablespoons minced shallots

Salt and pepper

In a saucepan fitted with a steamer, steam the salmon for 15 minutes, adding more water to the pan if necessary.

In a glass bowl, mash the salmon, tofu, capers, and shallots with a fork until the mixture achieves a spreadlike consistency but not a paste. Season to taste with salt and pepper.

STUFFED CHERRY TOMATOES 8 SERVINGS

Choose large cherry tomatoes for this recipe. If you prefer, you can use plum tomatoes or whatever small tomato is in season.

16 cherry tomatoes, halved and seeded

Salt and pepper

Tuna Spread (page 20)

Alfalfa sprouts

2 tablespoons minced parsley

Drain the cherry tomatoes, flesh-side down, on paper towels for 5 minutes, then season to taste with salt and pepper. Fill with the tuna spread. Arrange them on a platter over a bed of alfalfa sprouts and sprinkle with the parsley. Refrigerate for 30 minutes. Serve cold.

TUNA SPREAD ROLL-UPS 8 SERVINGS

Fresh steamed tuna has a much firmer texture and is less watery than canned. Even though the tuna here is used in a spread, you'll be much happier with the flavor.

Preheat the oven to 400°F.

Place the tortillas on a baking sheet and bake them for 2 minutes to make them just a little bit crispy. (Note that if you bake the tortillas longer than that they will break when you try to roll them.)

Spread the tuna mixture on three quarters of each tortilla, then layer on the onions, arugula, and cilantro.

Fold the bare bottom section of the tortilla over the filling and roll upward into a tight cylinder (see illustration on page 18).

Cut the rolls on the bias in quarters. To serve, arrange the little spirals on a plate over a bed of greens or alfalfa sprouts.

8 corn tortillas

Tuna Spread (recipe follows)

2 small Vidalia onions, sliced

4 cups arugula

¾ cup minced cilantro

TUNA SPREAD 8 SERVINGS

In a saucepan fitted with a steamer, steam the tuna for 15 minutes, adding more water if necessary.

In a glass bowl, mash the tuna steak, mayonnaise, olives, and onion with a fork until the mixture achieves a spreadlike consistency but not a paste. Season to taste with salt and pepper.

8 ounces fresh tuna steak

½ cup soy mayonnaise

¼ cup black olives (kalamata), pitted and minced

½ Spanish onion, minced

Salt and pepper

ROASTED GARLIC AND TOFU SPREAD 8 SERVINGS

This a simple spread that can be used as a dip for vegetables or on crackers. It is also an alternative spread for the roll-ups on pages 18, 20, and 25.

1 head of garlic

1 tablespoon olive oil

1 tablespoon dried oregano

Salt and pepper

One 8-ounce block soft tofu

½ cup minced chives

Preheat the oven to 400°F.

Cut off the top of the garlic head so that the cloves are exposed. Drizzle the oil on top. Sprinkle with the oregano and salt and pepper to taste. Place the garlic in a garlic roaster or wrap it in aluminum foil. Roast the garlic for about 20 minutes, or until the cloves are very soft.

Remove from the oven; using the blade of a chef's knife, squeeze the garlic cloves out of their papery skins. They should have the consistency of a paste. Reserve.

In a bowl, mash the tofu with a rubber spatula. Add the garlic paste and chives. Adjust the seasoning and mix well.

CHICKEN ROLL-UPS 4 SERVINGS

This recipe also works well with the Herbed Oven-Dried Tomatoes on page 71. Simply use them in place of the plum tomatoes.

2 tablespoons olive oil

8 garlic cloves, thinly sliced

4 flour tortillas

2 tablespoons Dijon mustard

4 Chicken Cutlets, sliced (recipe follows)

2 cups baby spinach leaves

4 small plum tomatoes, sliced

Preheat the oven to 400°F.

In a small skillet over medium heat, heat the oil and sauté the garlic until golden.

Place the tortillas on a baking sheet and bake them for 2 minutes to make them just a little bit crispy. (Note that if you bake the tortillas longer than that they will break when you try to roll them.)

Spread the mustard over three quarters of each tortilla. Lay the sliced chicken over the tortillas, then do the same with the spinach, tomatoes, and garlic.

Fold the bare bottom section of the tortilla over the filling and roll upward into a tight cylinder (see illustration on page 18).

Cut the rolls on the bias in quarters and serve the little spirals over a bed of greens or alfalfa sprouts.

CHICKEN CUTLETS 4 SERVINGS

2 tablespoons olive oil

2 tablespoons minced ginger

2 tablespoons minced rosemary

Salt and pepper to taste

4 chicken cutlets, trimmed of all fat

Rub all the ingredients on the chicken cutlets. In a medium sauté pan over medium heat, sauté the cutlets until golden brown, about 4 minutes on each side. Slice in thin strips.

SPRING ROLLS 5 SERVINGS

I like to serve these as hors d'oeuvres at parties. You can buy rice paper wrappers in the ethnic section of almost any big supermarket these days. Rice paper comes in packages of 20 sheets, which should serve about 5 people.

4 tablespoons olive oil

3 tablespoons minced ginger

3 garlic cloves, minced

1 large green pepper, seeded and cut into 3-inch-long julienne strips

1 large red pepper, seeded and cut into 3-inch-long julienne strips

1 medium carrot, peeled and cut into 3-inch-long julienne strips

1 medium yellow squash, cut into 3-inch-long julienne strips

1 bunch scallions, halved lengthwise and cut into 3-inch-long julienne strips

½ cup white wine

3 tablespoons minced kaffir lime leaves (or substitute 3 tablespoons minced lemongrass, 1 tablespoon grated lime zest, or 3 tablespoons lime juice)

2 tablespoons minced cilantro

Salt and pepper

1 package rice paper wrappers (about 20)

In a large skillet over high heat, add 3 tablespoons of the oil, the ginger, and the garlic and sauté for 1 minute. Add all the vegetables and sauté for 2 minutes, until tender but still crisp. Add the white wine and cook for 2 minutes more. Reserve and let cool. Add the minced kaffir lime leaves and cilantro. Season with salt and pepper to taste.

Immerse one sheet of rice paper in warm water for 15 seconds. Gently transfer to a flat surface and arrange some of the cooked vegetables on the center of the sheet (see illustration on page 18). Roll it up and transfer the roll to a cookie sheet lined with parchment paper. After you've made 10 rolls, preheat the oven to 500°F., then make the remaining 10.

Brush the rolls with the remaining 1 tablespoon olive oil and bake them for 5 minutes. Let them cool and cut on the diagonal. Serve with Soy-Ginger Dressing (page 60) for dipping.

SOUPS

My boss, Michael Fuchs, has said, "Luiz can make good soup from dirty socks." Okay, so maybe that's not very appealing, but seriously, while soups should not be an afterthought, they don't have to be complicated either. Warm in winter and refreshing in summer, soups should always be light and easy to digest.

BLACK BEAN SOUP 8 SERVINGS

I prefer to start from scratch and use fresh beans, even though it takes longer because they need to soak overnight. Some people like to use canned black beans, but they're high in sodium and weak in flavor. It's important to add the salt at the end of the cooking, not only because the liquid will be reduced throughout the cooking time, but also because the beans will shrink and become a little tough if it is added too soon.

Sort the beans carefully, discarding any pebbles and beans that are broken or discolored. Rinse. Transfer the beans to a bowl and cover generously with cold water. Let the beans stand overnight. Rinse again and drain.

In a medium stockpot over high heat, bring the vegetable stock to a rapid boil. Add the bay leaves and beans. Boil, uncovered, for 45 minutes. Using a slotted spoon, periodically skim off the foam that comes up from the beans.

In a large saucepan over medium heat, add the olive oil and sauté the onion until translucent. Add the garlic and jalapeño and sauté for 1 more minute. At this point, start to transfer the cooked beans from the stockpot to the saucepan, little by little so that they are coated in the garlic and jalapeño, always stirring with a wooden spoon. Discard the bay leaves. Adjust the heat to low.

Transfer one quarter of the bean mixture to a food processor and purée until smooth.

Bring the puréed beans back to the pan. Add the remaining vegetable stock, the cumin, chives, and parsley. Add salt and pepper to taste and simmer for 10 minutes, or until the soup is well flavored and thickened to your taste.

2 pounds uncooked black beans

6 cups Vegetable Stock (page 167)

4 bay leaves

2 tablespoons olive oil

1 medium Spanish onion, minced

4 garlic cloves, minced

1 jalapeño pepper, minced, with seeds

½ teaspoon ground cumin

2 tablespoons minced chives

2 tablespoons minced parsley

Salt and pepper

BUTTERNUT SQUASH SOUP 8 SERVINGS

This is a fall and winter favorite that is rich tasting without the use of cream or butter.

6 cups Vegetable Stock (page 167)

1 medium butternut squash, peeled and diced

1 leek stalk, just the white part, minced

2 tablespoons olive oil

1 shallot, minced

3 garlic cloves, minced

1 small zucchini, diced

1 small yellow squash, diced

2 tablespoons minced thyme

Salt and pepper

In a medium stockpot over high heat, add the stock and bring it to a boil. Lower the heat to medium, add the butternut squash and leek, and simmer them in the vegetable stock for 10 minutes. Check to see if they are softened by poking with a knife. Reserve one quarter of the squash for later use. Let the vegetable stock mixture cool off a little bit, then purée the vegetables in a blender with half the stock. Reserve the rest of the stock for later use.

In a large saucepan over medium heat, add the oil and sauté the shallot and garlic for 2 minutes. Add the remaining butternut squash, the zucchini, and yellow squash and sauté for 2 minutes. Add the thyme and transfer the puréed squash and vegetable broth to the saucepan. Cook for another 5 minutes and season to taste with salt and pepper.

CALDO VERDE 8 SERVINGS

Caldo Verde is a hearty soup that can be found in any small café in Portugal. The original recipe calls for sausage. I prefer to use chicken because it is lower in fat and blends so well with the other ingredients, but feel free to omit it if you prefer a vegetarian version. The greens in this recipe are high in nutrients and add a complex, peppery flavor to the broth.

In a large saucepan over medium heat, add the oil and brown the chicken on all sides, about 6 minutes. Add the onion and garlic and sauté for 2 minutes, or until the onion is translucent. Add the potatoes and stock and cook for 30 minutes. At this point the potatoes should be very soft and well blended with the stock. You can mash them using the back of a wooden spoon (or keep them lumpy if you prefer).

Reduce the heat to low. Add 2 cups of water and all the greens and cook for 10 more minutes, or until they are wilted. Season to taste with salt and pepper and turn the heat off. Cover, let rest for 10 minutes, and serve.

2 tablespoons olive oil

4 boneless chicken thighs, trimmed of fat and cut into chunks

½ medium Spanish onion, chopped

4 garlic cloves, minced

4 medium russet potatoes, peeled and cubed

6 cups Vegetable Stock (page 167) or Chicken Stock (page 162)

2 cups spinach

2 cups thickly sliced collard greens or kale

2 cups coarsely chopped watercress

2 cups thickly sliced Savoy cabbage

½ cup coarsely chopped parsley

Salt and pepper

CORN SOUP 4 SERVINGS

This is a quick, creamless soup that is blended, creating a surprisingly thick and smooth consistency.

2 tablespoons olive oil

2 shallots, minced

4 garlic cloves, minced

2 cups corn kernels (2 large cobs)

4 cups Chicken Stock (page 162)

Salt and pepper

3 tablespoons minced chives

In a large saucepan over medium-high heat, add the oil and sauté the shallots and garlic for 2 minutes. Add the corn kernels and sauté for 2 minutes more. Add 2 cups of the chicken stock and bring to a simmer, about 5 minutes. Turn the heat off and let it cool a bit.

Working in batches, transfer the corn-broth mixture to a blender and purée well.

Place the puréed corn back in the saucepan and turn the heat to medium. Add the remaining 2 cups of stock and bring to a simmer. Season to taste with salt and pepper and cook for 5 minutes, always stirring with a wooden spoon. (Puréeing the corn kernels releases all their starch, while the cooking and stirring blends the starch into the broth.) Add the chives and serve immediately.

TOMATO GAZPACHO 8 SERVINGS

For this recipe I use homemade tomato sauce and juice extracted from fresh tomatoes by a juicer. But you can substitute a good brand of tomato juice if you need to save time.

In a large saucepan over high heat, heat the oil, then sauté the onion, garlic, green pepper, yellow pepper, and tomatoes for 1 minute. Add the tomato sauce and juice and a good pinch of sugar (it helps to break the acidity of the tomatoes). Cook for 10 minutes, stirring, until the tomato flesh is broken down; let cool. Season with the pepper and salt to taste.

Add the cucumber, scallions, cilantro or parsley, and chives. Transfer everything to a glass or stainless steel bowl and cover with plastic wrap. Refrigerate for 2 hours and serve.

2 tablespoons olive oil

½ Spanish onion, minced

4 garlic cloves, minced

¼ cup seeded and finely diced green pepper

¼ cup seeded and finely diced yellow pepper

4 plum tomatoes, seeded and coarsely chopped

1 cup Tomato Sauce (page 166)

2 cups tomato juice

Pinch of sugar

1 tablespoon black pepper

Salt

½ cup peeled and finely diced cucumber

4 scallion stalks, both white and green sections, minced

½ cup minced cilantro or parsley

½ cup minced chives

ESCAROLE AND BEAN SOUP 4 SERVINGS

With two types of beans, red and white, this green escarole soup is a true Italian patriot. Adding the greens at the end preserves their fresh color and crispness.

Sort the beans carefully, discarding any pebbles and beans that are broken or discolored. Place in a bowl and cover generously with water. Soak overnight, then rinse and drain. Reserve.

In a large saucepan over medium heat, add the olive oil and sauté the onion, garlic, and celery for 3 minutes, or until cooked through. Add the beans and sauté for 3 minutes. Add the stock and cook for 30 minutes, or until the beans are tender. Remove from the heat, pour into a large bowl, and stir in the escarole. Season to taste with salt and pepper and serve immediately.

1 cup red kidney beans, soaked overnight

1 cup cannellini beans, soaked overnight

2 tablespoons olive oil

1 medium Spanish onion, chopped

3 garlic cloves, minced

3 tablespoons thinly sliced celery

6 cups Vegetable Stock (page 167)

4 cups chopped escarole

Salt and pepper

LENTIL SOUP 4 SERVINGS

This is simple, healthy, and filling and particularly good as a main dish, served with a hearty salad.

6 cups Chicken Stock (page 162) or Vegetable Stock (page 167)

2 cups lentils

2 bay leaves

2 tablespoons olive oil

1 medium Spanish onion, chopped

2 garlic cloves, minced

1 large carrot, peeled, quartered lengthwise, and cut into ½-inch segments

1 large zucchini, peeled, quartered lengthwise, and cut into ½-inch segments

4 plum tomatoes, chopped

Salt and pepper

¼ cup minced parsley

In a large saucepan over medium heat, add the stock, lentils, and bay leaves and simmer, uncovered, for 10 minutes, or until the lentils are tender.

Meanwhile, in a skillet over high heat, add the olive oil and sauté the onion and garlic for 3 minutes, or until the onion is translucent. Add the carrot and zucchini and cook for 5 minutes, or until cooked through. Transfer the skillet's contents to the saucepan with the lentils. Add the tomatoes and cook 20 minutes longer, or until the tomato flesh has broken down.

Take about 2 cups of the soup mixture and purée (see Note) in a blender. Return the puréed mixture back to the saucepan and stir in. Season with salt and pepper to taste and add the parsley.

NOTE: Be very careful when puréeing hot ingredients (lentils in this case) because they are likely to explode out of the blender. Place a kitchen towel on top of the lid and apply pressure while turning the blender on. Another alternative is simply to let the liquid cool first. You can do this by adding a few ice cubes prior to blending.

ROASTED BEET SOUP 4 SERVINGS

When you roast the beets and fennel, the flavor becomes sweeter and more prominent, and that's the base of this soup. Much like a borscht, it can be served either hot or chilled.

2 large beets

1 large fennel bulb

2 tablespoons olive oil

1 red onion, chopped

2 garlic cloves

5 cups Chicken Stock (page 162) or Vegetable Stock (page 167)

2 tablespoons minced parsley

2 tablespoons chopped dill

Salt and pepper

Preheat the oven to 350°F.

Wash the beets and fennel carefully, trim them, and cut in half lengthwise. Place them on a baking dish lined with parchment paper and bake for 40 minutes. Let them cool off, then peel and dice them.

In a medium skillet over high heat, add the olive oil and sauté the onion and garlic for 3 minutes, or until the onion is translucent. Add the vegetables, reduce the heat, and cook the vegetables for 5 minutes more.

In a blender, add the sautéed vegetables and 1 cup of the stock. Carefully purée (see Note) all the ingredients.

In a medium saucepan over medium heat, add the remaining 4 cups of stock and the puréed vegetables. Simmer, uncovered, for 20 minutes, or until reduced slightly and the flavors are incorporated. Add the parsley and dill and season with salt and pepper to taste. Serve hot or chilled.

NOTE: Be very careful when puréeing hot ingredients because they are likely to explode out of the blender. Place a kitchen towel on top of the lid and apply pressure while turning the blender on. Another alternative is simply to let the liquid cool first. You can do this by adding a few ice cubes prior to blending.

MISO SOUP 4 SERVINGS

This classic Japanese soup is actually quite easy to make. The kelp has cleansing properties, and I recommend it as a post-caipirinhas hangover cure.

In a large saucepan over medium heat, add the stock, diluted miso, and kelp and cook, uncovered, for 10 minutes. Add the tofu and scallions and serve immediately.

NOTE: If using dried kelp, soak it in warm water for at least 2 hours before using.

5 cups Chicken Stock (page 162) or Vegetable Stock (page 167)

2 tablespoons white miso diluted in ¼ cup water

1 cup kelp (see Note), cut into bite-size pieces

Four ½-inch slices firm tofu, diced

8 scallion stalks, thinly sliced, green part only

CROUTONS 4 SERVINGS

It's always nice to serve croutons or bread with soup. Feel free to use any kind of bread you like, but Ezekiel bread is unique because it is flourless and all the grains used to make it are sprouted.

2 tablespoons minced onion or garlic

2 tablespoons olive oil

1 tablespoon minced oregano, rosemary, or parsley

4 slices sesame Ezekiel bread, diced

1 teaspoon salt

In a large sauté pan over high heat, sauté the onion or garlic in the olive oil for 2 minutes. Add the herb of your choice and sauté for 1 minute more. Add the bread and salt and sauté, shaking the skillet so that all the bread dices are coated with oil, until the bread is golden brown, about 3 minutes.

ZUCCHINI, CHICKEN, AND MUSHROOM SOUP 4 SERVINGS

Everyone knows that chicken soup is a great remedy. My version of this home-cooking classic has an Italian accent. (I don't have an Italian grandmother, but I can pretend.)

6 cups Chicken Stock (page 162)

2 skinless and boneless chicken breasts

2 tablespoons olive oil

1 small Spanish onion, chopped

5 garlic cloves, minced

1 large zucchini, quartered lengthwise, then cut into ½-inch segments

2 cups quartered white mushrooms

2 tomatoes, diced

½ cup white wine

½ cup minced chives

Salt and pepper

In a large stockpot over high heat, bring the chicken stock to a boil. Add the chicken and cook for 5 minutes, or until just cooked through. Remove from the heat, remove the chicken, and reserve the stockpot of liquid. After the chicken has cooled, shred the meat by hand and reserve.

In a large skillet over high heat, heat the olive oil, then sauté the onion and garlic for 2 minutes. Add the shredded chicken and sauté for 3 minutes. Add the zucchini, mushrooms, and tomatoes and sauté for 3 minutes, then add the white wine and cook for 3 minutes. Add 2 cups water and scrape the bottom of the skillet with a wooden spoon to incorporate all the flavors.

Add the ingredients in the skillet to the stockpot with the chicken broth. Bring to a simmer over medium-high heat and cook, stirring constantly for 5 minutes, or until hot. Add the chives, season to taste with salt and pepper, and cook for 3 minutes more.

SALADS AND GRAINS

Salads are the healthiest of foods; they lighten the rest of the meal as well as add a decorative element. I encourage you to play with the presentation of my recipes and consider serving green salads after the main course, as the Italians do, to aid in digestion. On the other hand, grains can be vibrant with the proper seasoning. Such additions as sweet dried fruit or nuts complement the innate nuttiness of the grains.

BROCCOLINI AND CHAYOTE PASTA SALAD 8 SERVINGS

Frequently the problem with pasta salad is that you have to continually reseason it, making it difficult to prepare ahead of time. I have solved that problem in this recipe by dressing the pasta while it is still warm and can absorb the flavors and by using ginger and lime, which impart a pleasing, enduring zestiness.

In a large pot of boiling water, cook the pasta until al dente, according to package directions. In a steamer, steam the vegetables until just cooked through, about 5 minutes.

While the pasta and vegetables are cooking, prepare the marinade. In a large glass or stainless steel bowl, whisk all the ingredients together well.

Toss the pasta and vegetables in the bowl with the marinade. Season to taste with salt and pepper and add the cilantro. Refrigerate for at least 30 minutes before serving.

1 pound bow tie, spiral, or penne pasta

1 bunch broccolini, the tough part of the stems cut off

2 carrots, peeled, quartered lengthwise, and cut into 1-inch segments

2 chayotes, peeled, pitted, and cut into bite-size chunks

MARINADE

3 tablespoons white vinegar

4 tablespoons olive oil

Juice of 1 lime

1 red onion, cut in half, then thinly sliced

5 garlic cloves, minced

3 tablespoons minced ginger

Salt and pepper

1 cup minced cilantro

CHICKEN SALAD SALPICAO 8 SERVINGS

This is my mother's version of a common Brazilian dish. It can be served as a first course, a main course for a luncheon, or as a side dish at a barbecue alongside green salad and corn on the cob.

2 skinless, boneless chicken breasts, trimmed of any fat

2 tablespoons olive oil

1 medium Spanish onion, minced

5 garlic cloves

½ cup white wine

Salt and pepper

1 large carrot, grated

½ cup raisins

½ cup soy mayonnaise or egg-yolk mayonnaise (page 168)

½ cup minced parsley

2 cups Potato Sticks (page 171)

In a saucepan of boiling water, poach the chicken for 10 minutes. Cool the chicken, then shred the meat by hand.

In a skillet over high heat, add the olive oil and sauté the onion and garlic for 2 minutes, or until the onion is translucent. Add the chicken and sauté until it starts to get a bit "crispy" and golden around the edges, about 5 minutes. Add the wine and deglaze (see page 4) the pan. Season with salt and pepper to taste and let it cool completely.

In a medium bowl, combine the chicken, carrot, raisins, mayonnaise, and parsley. Mix well. The mixture should be moist but not soggy. Refrigerate.

Just before serving, mix in the potato sticks.

HONEY MUSTARD DRESSING MAKES 2 ½ CUPS

This is yet another creamy dressing that completely avoids the use of cream, cheese, or oil. The yogurt tempers the acidity of the vinegars and mustard while providing a smooth, thick texture.

In a blender, mix well the mustard, yogurt, and balsamic and red wine vinegars. Pour the mixture into a bowl. Add the parsley, season to taste with salt and pepper, and whisk well. Serve cold.

¼ cup honey mustard

¼ cup nonfat plain yogurt

¼ cup balsamic vinegar

¼ cup red wine vinegar

½ cup minced parsley

Salt and pepper

PAPAYA DRESSING MAKES 1 ½ CUPS

This dressing goes nicely with arugula salads.

In a blender, purée all the ingredients.

1 cup sliced papaya

¼ medium red onion, minced

4 basil leaves, minced

½ cup white vinegar

Salt and pepper to taste

PEANUT, TOFU, AND ROASTED ONION DRESSING MAKES 3 CUPS

This dressing is fantastic with spinach or arugula. The peanuts and tofu create a very creamy consistency without the use of oil or mayonnaise.

½ cup skinless roasted peanuts

½ cup Roasted Onions (page 57)

8 ounces soft tofu

¾ cup balsamic vinegar

¼ cup minced parsley

Salt and pepper to taste

Grind the peanuts very fine in the food processor, then add the other ingredients and process well. Serve cold.

COLESLAW 8 SERVINGS

I tried coleslaw for the first time in a diner a few years ago. It really wasn't good—mushy vegetables soaked in a thin sauce—but I liked the sweet, sour, and tangy combination of flavors. My version uses crisp, fresh vegetables, very thinly sliced and very lightly dressed. This colorful, vibrant salad is now one of my favorite recipes, and has almost eclipsed that first inauspicious encounter.

In a large mixing bowl, combine all the ingredients, following the sequence in the ingredient list. Refrigerate, covered, for at least 30 minutes. Serve cold.

2 cups thinly sliced green cabbage leaves

2 cups thinly sliced red cabbage leaves

2 cups grated carrots

½ medium Vidalia onion, thinly sliced

1 tablespoon minced garlic

1 tablespoon minced ginger

2 tablespoons soy mayonnaise

1 tablespoon white vinegar

1 tablespoon sugar

5 tablespoons minced parsley

Salt and pepper to taste

VIBRANT SLAW SALAD 4 SERVINGS

Crunchy, sweet, and colorful, this salad is yet another improvement on diner coleslaw.

2 cups thinly sliced red cabbage

1 medium carrot, shredded

2 cups halved green grapes

1 cup unsalted roasted cashews

4 scallion stalks, chopped

4 tablespoons minced parsley

In a bowl, mix all the ingredients well and refrigerate for at least 30 minutes. Serve cold.

WILD RICE AND VEGETABLE SALAD 4 SERVINGS

I have served this recipe many times at large parties (once to a roomful of cops), and it is as popular with health nuts as it is with basic meat-and-potato lovers. One of the secrets to its success is in the marinating process—marinating the vegetables while they are still warm locks in the flavor and eliminates the need for additional dressing later.

In a saucepan over medium heat, "toast" the rice (see page 5), stirring constantly, for 2 minutes. Add the boiling water and cook, covered, for 40 minutes, or until the rice is tender. Check periodically, skimming off the foam when it gathers around the edges and adding more water if necessary.

In a large pot fitted with a steam basket, steam the carrots, soybeans, and broccolini for 5 minutes, or until cooked through but still crisp.

While steaming the vegetables, add the marinade ingredients to a large nonreactive bowl. Whisk well.

Transfer the steamed vegetables and cooked rice to the marinade bowl and toss gently. Cover with plastic wrap and refrigerate for 15 minutes before serving.

1 cup wild rice

3 cups boiling water

2 carrots, peeled, steamed, and quartered lengthwise, then cut into ½-inch pieces

1 cup fresh soybeans (edamame), shelled

1 cup broccolini florets

MARINADE

Juice of 1 lime

2 tablespoons olive oil

1 tablespoon white vinegar

1 small Vidalia onion, thinly sliced

1 tablespoon minced ginger

Salt and pepper to taste

SIMPLE SALAD 4 SERVINGS

This recipe is so easy to make, it can't go by any other name. I first tasted this combination in a restaurant in Hawaii and was impressed with how nicely the flavors of the roasted onions and the soy-ginger dressing blend together.

ROASTED ONIONS

1 large Vidalia onion, sliced ⅛ inch thick in a horseshoe shape

1 tablespoon olive oil

Salt

1 head Boston lettuce

2 plum tomatoes, sliced

Soy-Ginger Dressing (page 60)

Preheat the oven to 250°F.

In a large bowl, add the onion slices, oil, and salt to taste. Toss well so all the onion slices are coated.

Transfer the onions to a baking sheet lined with parchment paper. Bake for 20 to 25 minutes. As the onions start to get some color, move them around or flip them over. Leave them in the oven for another 10 minutes, or until golden brown. Transfer the onions to a plate and place in the freezer for about 15 minutes.

For presentation, the trick is to build some volume on the plate when you serve it: Keep the lettuce leaves whole, arrange the tomatoes on top of the lettuce, arrange the onions around the edge, and sprinkle the dressing on top.

SOY-GINGER DRESSING MAKES ¾ CUP

This is a sweet, pungent (and oil-less) dressing. It is a perfect accompaniment for the Simple Salad (page 57) and also goes very well with Spring Rolls (page 27).

In a small bowl, whisk together all the ingredients.	½ cup low-sodium soy sauce
	2 tablespoons grated ginger, with juice
	¼ cup white vinegar
	2 tablespoons sugar

CHERRY DRESSING MAKES 1¾ CUPS

This dressing is delicious drizzled over sliced tomato and onions.

In a blender, purée all the ingredients.	1 cup pitted cherries
	¼ cup chopped Vidalia onion
	3 scallion stalks, green part only, sliced
	½ cup red wine vinegar
	Salt and pepper to taste

BROWN RICE WITH CASHEW NUTS AND CRANBERRIES

8 SERVINGS

A lot of people don't like brown rice, but many of those people have only eaten bland, dry versions bought at health food stores. This recipe is seasoned with onions, garlic, and ginger and combines the crunchy texture of cashew nuts, the tartness of cranberries, and the fresh flavors of parsley and scallions.

1 pound Lundberg brown rice

2 tablespoons canola oil

½ Spanish onion, chopped

2 tablespoons minced ginger

3 garlic cloves, minced

1 cup dried cranberries

1 cup roasted unsalted cashew nuts

   Salt

½ cup minced parsley

3 scallion stalks, sliced

In a large saucepan, "toast" the rice (see page 5) over high heat for 1 minute, stirring constantly so it doesn't burn. Add 4 cups water and cook, uncovered, for 30 minutes, or until the rice is tender. Skim off the foam as it collects, adding more water if needed. Drain through a strainer and reserve.

In a large skillet over high heat, add the oil and sauté the onion for 2 minutes. Add the ginger and sauté for 1 minute, then add the garlic and cranberries and sauté for 2 minutes more, or until cooked through. Add the reserved rice, cashew nuts, and salt to taste. Keep stirring for 30 seconds. Turn the heat off, then add the parsley and scallions. Serve immediately.

QUINOA TABBOULEH 8 SERVINGS

Tabbouleh is a Middle Eastern salad that is traditionally made with bulgur wheat. I substitute quinoa in my version. Quinoa is an ancient South American grain that is high in protein and not as heavy in consistency as bulgur.

In a medium saucepan over high heat, add the quinoa and "toast" the grain (see page 5) for 2 minutes. Add 2 cups water and bring it to a boil. Reduce the heat to low and simmer, covered, for 15 minutes, or until the quinoa is soft and the water has been absorbed. Transfer the quinoa to a bowl to cool.

In a large bowl, mix together all the other ingredients except the lettuces. Stir in the cooled quinoa. Refrigerate for 30 minutes.

Add the lettuces, mix well, and serve immediately.

1 cup quinoa

2 tablespoons olive oil

½ cup lime juice

½ medium red onion, minced

2 garlic cloves, minced

½ cup minced parsley

½ cup minced mint

3 plum tomatoes, seeded and diced

1 cup peeled, seeded, and diced cucumber (approximately 1 medium cucumber)

Salt and pepper to taste

2 cups thinly sliced red leaf lettuce

2 cups thinly sliced green leaf lettuce

BLUEBERRY AND BALSAMIC DRESSING MAKES 1 ½ CUPS

I like to serve this dressing with mesclun.

1 cup blueberries

1 garlic clove, minced

2 tablespoons minced parsley

¾ cup balsamic vinegar

Salt and pepper to taste

In a blender, purée all the ingredients.

PINEAPPLE DRESSING MAKES 1 ¾ CUPS

I like to serve this on spinach salads. The yellow and green reminds me of the Brazilian flag.

1 cup sliced sweet pineapple

1 tablespoon minced ginger

2 tablespoons minced cilantro

½ cup lime juice

Salt and pepper to taste

In a blender, purée all the ingredients.

VEGETABLES

Eat your vegetables...because they're delicious. In restaurants, vegetables tend to be second class to meat and I find this offensive. They can be stars too. Many of my vegetable recipes can hold their own as a main dish; they're also flexible and complement many menus. Give vegetables a chance—the more you eat, the more you'll like them. This is coming from someone who hated spinach once upon a time. So throw out your childhood prejudices and dive in.

ASPARAGUS AND ROASTED RED PEPPERS 4 SERVINGS

Plain steamed asparagus lacks personality, but the red peppers and sesame oil give this dish new life. Don't be intimidated by the roasting of the red pepper. It's much easier than you might think, and the flavor is far superior to that of bottled peppers.

Holding an asparagus stalk by both the bottom and the tip, bend gently until it breaks. The top part should be two thirds of the stalk's regular size. Discard the bottom part because it is tough to eat. Peel the skin of the stalk just below the crown, as you would do with carrots. Do the same with all the stalks. Using a steam basket, steam the stalks for 10 minutes. Reserve.

Brush 1 teaspoon of sesame oil over the red pepper. Over a high flame, roast the pepper, turning it after the skin is burned. When the whole vegetable is blackened, put it in a paper bag for 5 minutes. Peel off all the burned skin while holding the pepper under cold running water. Cut off the top, discard all the seeds, and cut the pepper into ¼-inch-thick strips.

In a large nonstick skillet over medium heat, toast the sesame seeds until they start to turn golden. Add the remaining 1 teaspoon sesame oil, the asparagus stalks, and the pepper strips. Sauté 2 minutes and season to taste with salt and pepper. Serve immediately.

20 asparagus stalks

2 teaspoons sesame oil

1 large sweet red pepper

1 tablespoon sesame seeds

Salt and pepper

COLLARD GREENS 8 SERVINGS

This side dish holds an important place in Brazilian cooking. Traditionally it is served with feijoada, a black bean and pork stew that is the Brazilian national dish, adding fiber and nutrients to the meal. It's also a great accompaniment for roast chicken.

1 tablespoon olive oil

2 garlic cloves, minced

1½ pounds collard greens, mustard greens, or kale, thinly sliced

Salt

In a large nonstick skillet over high heat, add the olive oil and sauté the garlic for 1 minute, until the oil is infused with garlic. Add the greens and toss to coat them well with the garlic and olive oil, sautéing for only 2 to 3 minutes, just until tender. Season with salt to taste and serve immediately.

HERBED OVEN-DRIED TOMATOES 8 SERVINGS

I prefer these sweet, slightly moist dried tomatoes to sun-dried tomatoes, which can be overly pungent and require rehydration (if they are not packed in oil already). I have chosen parsley, oregano, and thyme, but any herbs may be used, such as rosemary, chives, sage, or cilantro. You can serve these tomatoes in salads, pasta, or sandwiches.

12 plum tomatoes, halved

2 cups parsley, with stems

2 cups oregano, with sprigs

2 cups thyme, with sprigs

4 garlic cloves, sliced

Salt and pepper

2 tablespoons olive oil

Preheat the oven to 200°F. or the lowest temperature on your oven.

Set the tomatoes in a shallow baking dish or baking sheet lined with parchment paper. Arrange the herbs and garlic on top of the tomatoes. Season to taste with salt and pepper, drizzle on some olive oil, and cook overnight, or at least 8 hours, depending on how dry you want them.

JAPANESE EGGPLANT 4 SERVINGS

I first tried a version of this recipe in an Asian restaurant in New York. However tasty, it was loaded with sugar, oil, and fat. I took the sugar out, lowered the amount of oil, and added fresh ginger, with equally tasty results.

In a wok, heat the oil over high heat. Add the shallots and sauté for 1 minute. Add the ginger and Thai pepper and sauté for 1 more minute. Add the eggplant slices and cook for 2 minutes, or until softened, tossing well to coat the eggplant with all the flavors in the pan. Add the soy sauce and ¼ cup water, reduce the heat to medium, and cook for 8 minutes more, or until the eggplant is very tender. Garnish with the scallions and serve immediately.

2 tablespoons canola oil

2 shallots, minced

2 tablespoons minced ginger

1 small dried Thai pepper, minced, with seeds, or ½ jalapeño without the seeds

1 pound Japanese eggplant, sliced about ½ inch thick on the bias

2 tablespoons soy sauce

4 scallion stalks, cut on the bias into ½-inch segments

GARBANZO BEAN, SPINACH, AND SHIITAKE MUSHROOM TART 5 SERVINGS

If you're looking for an alternative vegetable side dish, these tarts are high in nutrition and low in fat. Place them on a bed of greens for an attractive presentation.

One 8-ounce can organic garbanzo beans

2 tablespoons olive oil

½ medium Vidalia onion, minced

3 garlic cloves, minced

1 cup sliced shiitake mushrooms

3 cups baby spinach

Salt and pepper

½ cup minced chives

½ tablespoon sesame oil

1 small Thai pepper, minced

⅓ cup seasoned bread crumbs

2 egg whites

Preheat the oven to 350°F.

Purée the garbanzo beans in a food processor and reserve.

In a large skillet over high heat, heat the oil. Add the onion and sauté until golden brown, about 3 minutes. Add the garlic and sauté for 1 minute. Add the mushrooms and sauté for 3 minutes, or until soft, always shaking the pan so they don't burn. Add the spinach and sauté for 2 minutes, or until the spinach is wilted. Season with some salt so the mushrooms release some water. Add the garbanzo bean purée and mix well. Season to taste with salt and pepper and add the chives, sesame oil, and Thai pepper. Transfer to a bowl and let cool.

Grease five ½-cup ramekins with olive oil and coat them lightly with the seasoned bread crumbs.

In a medium bowl, beat the egg whites until firm. Little by little, fold them gently into the garbanzo bean mixture with a rubber spatula. Fold the mixture into the ramekins.

Bake for 10 minutes on the lower rack of the oven. Let cool for 2 minutes, then invert right onto a serving plate.

GRILLED VEGETABLES 4 SERVINGS

The combined sweetness of the teriyaki sauce and the balsamic vinegar creates a delicious barbecue marinade for a summer vegetable harvest.

Preheat the grill.

In a large bowl, combine the garlic, thyme, parsley, olive oil, balsamic vinegar, teriyaki sauce, paprika, and salt and pepper to taste. Whisk well. Add the vegetables and marinate for 20 minutes. Grill the vegetables, reserving the marinade. If the grill is very hot, the grilling process should take no more than 5 minutes—the vegetables should remain crisp; you just want to give them some grill marks. Place the vegetables on a serving plate and drizzle the reserved marinade on top.

3 garlic cloves, minced

Leaves from 12 thyme sprigs, minced

2 tablespoons minced parsley

2 tablespoons olive oil

¼ cup balsamic vinegar

¼ cup teriyaki sauce

1 tablespoon paprika

Salt and pepper

1 medium eggplant, cut ¼ inch thick on the bias

1 large zucchini, cut ¼ inch thick on the bias

1 large yellow squash, cut ¼ inch thick on the bias

2 large red bell peppers, sliced ½ inch thick

MUSHROOM MEDLEY 4 SERVINGS

Depending on the mushrooms you choose for this recipe, it can be a simple dish for every day or a special accompaniment to a holiday meal. Portobello, white, and cremini mushrooms are suitable for casual meals, while the more expensive and harder-to-find morel, porcini, and oyster mushrooms add an exquisite sophistication for fancier occasions.

In a large nonstick skillet over high heat, add the oil and sauté the shallots and garlic for 3 minutes, or until the shallots are translucent. Reduce the heat to medium and add the mushrooms. Cook for about 8 minutes, shaking the pan to move them around, until the mushrooms are soft and browned. Add the wine and stock and cook for 2 minutes. Season to taste with salt and pepper and stir in the herbs. Serve immediately.

2 tablespoons olive oil

2 shallots, chopped

2 garlic cloves, minced

1 cup thinly sliced portobello mushrooms

1 cup thinly sliced shiitake mushrooms

1 cup thinly sliced white mushrooms

1 cup thinly sliced cremini mushrooms

½ cup white wine

½ cup chicken stock

Salt and pepper

4 tablespoons minced chives

2 tablespoons minced oregano

OKRA AND TOMATOES 4 SERVINGS

I add wheat germ to this dish because it boosts the nutritional content and adds a pleasant crunchiness. The coconut milk lends an exotic Brazilian flair, blending with the tomatoes to make an attractive pink sauce.

1 tablespoon olive oil

1 Spanish onion, chopped

4 garlic cloves, minced

1 small poblano pepper, seeded and chopped

1 pound okra, cut into ½-inch segments (see Note)

4 plum tomatoes, seeded and chopped

¼ cup shredded coconut

½ cup vegetable stock or white wine

½ cup soy milk

2 tablespoons wheat germ

2 tablespoons minced oregano

Salt and pepper

In a large nonstick skillet over high heat, heat the oil. Add the onion and sauté for 2 minutes, or until the onion is translucent. Add the garlic and poblano pepper and sauté for 2 minutes more, or until the pepper is softened. Add the okra, turn the heat down to medium, and cook for 5 minutes, or until they are tender. Add the tomatoes and coconut and cook for 5 minutes, or until they are softened. Add the stock or wine, soy milk, wheat germ, and oregano. Season to taste with salt and pepper and cook for 5 minutes more, or until the liquid reduces a little.

NOTE: If you prefer okra without the gelatinous texture the vegetable is famous for, before you cook the onion, cook the okra for 5 minutes in a skillet over high heat, stirring with a wooden spoon. The gum will stick to the side of the skillet. Reserve the okra until you need to use it in the recipe.

BRAZILIAN OKRA WITH CILANTRO 4 SERVINGS

A lot of people don't like the gummy texture okra often has. The sautéing technique I use here removes the gumminess so that the okra is drier.

In a skillet over high heat, add the okra and cook for 5 minutes, always stirring with a wooden spoon so it doesn't burn. The okra's gum will stick to the sides of the pan. Transfer the okra to a plate and reserve.

In a nonstick skillet over medium heat, add the olive oil and sauté the onion and garlic for 3 to 4 minutes, or until the onion is translucent. Add the okra and cook for 5 minutes more, or until the okra just begins to be tender but is still crisp. Season to taste with salt and pepper, add the cilantro, and serve immediately.

1 pound okra, sliced into ½-inch segments

1 tablespoon olive oil

1 large red onion, chopped

2 garlic cloves, minced

Salt and pepper

½ cup minced cilantro

WHITE BEANS 8 SERVINGS

Instead of using the traditional pork fat and bacon to flavor the beans, I infuse oil with herbs and spices. I swear, serve these beans over rice and they sing.

2 cups white or cannellini beans

1 Spanish onion, chopped

1 tablespoon olive oil

2 garlic cloves, minced

1 Thai pepper, minced (optional)

2 scallion stalks, green part only, minced

2 tablespoons minced parsley

1 teaspoon ground cumin

4 cups Vegetable Stock (page 167)

3 bay leaves

Salt

Sort the beans carefully, discarding any stones. Place the beans in a bowl, cover with water, and soak overnight or for at least 12 hours. Drain and rinse. Reserve.

In a large saucepan over high heat, sauté the onion in the olive oil for 2 minutes, or until translucent. Add the garlic and sauté for 2 minutes more, or until the garlic starts to brown lightly. Add the Thai pepper, scallions, parsley, and cumin and sauté for 1 minute. Add the beans and cook for 2 minutes, stirring constantly with a wooden spoon.

Add the vegetable stock and the bay leaves, reduce the heat, and cook for 30 to 45 minutes, or until the beans are tender. Stir the mixture periodically and check to make sure the beans are not sticking to the bottom of the pan. Season to taste with salt while the beans are cooking. Let rest for 10 minutes before serving.

PEA PURÉE 8 SERVINGS

I serve this recipe with sautéed carrots, grilled chicken, fish, or anything else that's begging for a burst of garlicky green on the plate.

1 head of garlic

1 tablespoon minced fresh oregano

1 tablespoon olive oil

4 cups fresh peas

2 cups fat-free milk or soy milk

Salt and pepper

Preheat the oven to 400°F.

Cut off the top of a garlic head so that all the cloves are exposed. Sprinkle with the oregano and drizzle the olive oil on top. Place the garlic in a garlic roaster or wrap it in aluminum foil. Roast for 30 minutes. Using the blade of a chef's knife, squeeze the cloves out of their papery skins. They should have the consistency of a paste.

Meanwhile, in a saucepan of boiling water, cook the peas for 15 minutes, or until soft. Drain and transfer to a food processor. Purée well. Add the garlic paste and milk. Process again and season to taste with salt and pepper. Transfer the mixture back to the saucepan and cook over low heat until it achieves the consistency you like. Serve immediately.

PAD "NOT" THAI 4 SERVINGS

In my vegetarian version of this Thai dish, I have added Savoy cabbage and carrots and lowered the sodium. Make sure that your wok is well heated, and be vigilant and quick while you stir-fry, or you run the risk of your food sticking to the sides or losing its crunchiness.

In a large pot of boiling water, cook the noodles until just cooked through, according to the package instructions. Drain and reserve.

In a wok over high heat, add the oil and sauté the ginger for 1 minute. Add the garlic and Thai pepper and sauté for 1 minute more. Add the shiitake mushrooms and cook for 2 minutes, always stirring, until they are soft. Add the noodles, carrots, and cabbage and cook for an extra minute, until warmed through.

Keep stirring and add the vinegar, sugar, lime juice, paprika, soy sauce, and sprouts. Mix well with the vegetables and noodles and cook for only 1 minute. Turn off the heat.

Add the peanuts, scallions, and cilantro and serve immediately.

8 ounces rice noodles

2 tablespoons canola oil

2 tablespoons minced fresh ginger

2 garlic cloves, minced

1 Thai pepper, minced, with seeds

1 cup sliced shiitake mushrooms

½ cup shredded carrots

½ cup shredded Savoy cabbage

2 tablespoons rice vinegar

1 tablespoon sugar

Juice of 1 lime

1 tablespoon paprika

1 tablespoon soy sauce

1 cup bean sprouts

¼ cup roasted peanuts

¼ cup scallions

2 tablespoons minced cilantro

RED BEAN AND CHAYOTE SALAD 4 SERVINGS

Beans are eaten every day in Brazilian homes, and this salad is a favorite. Chayote, a viny plant commonly called "chu chu," grows wild with such singular ease and abandon that you can find it everywhere in Brazil. For such a common vegetable, it's amazing how uncommonly good it tastes.

2 cups red beans

2 chayotes

1 medium red onion, sliced

2 tablespoons white vinegar

2 tablespoons olive oil

Juice of 1 lime

1 cup halved cherry tomatoes

1 cup chopped cilantro

Salt and pepper

Sort the beans very carefully, discarding all the stones. Put the beans in a bowl and cover with 6 cups water. Soak overnight, or at least 12 hours. Rinse, drain, and transfer the beans to a saucepan. Add 6 cups water and cook for 45 minutes over medium heat, or until the beans are soft. As the beans cook, remove all the foam that comes from the boiling process, using a slotted spoon.

Peel the chayotes, cut them in half with a paring knife, and cut out the white pits. Dice the vegetable into ½-inch cubes. Steam for 10 minutes, or until tender.

While you're cooking the beans and steaming the chayote, in a large bowl, combine the red onion, vinegar, olive oil, and lime juice. Stir in the beans and chayote while they're still warm so that the vegetables will absorb the flavor of the marinade easily.

Stir in the tomatoes and cilantro and season with salt and pepper to taste. Refrigerate for 30 minutes before serving.

SPAGHETTI SQUASH WITH TOMATO SAUCE 4 SERVINGS

Sometimes I like to serve this dish with chicken that I shred by hand so that it blends with the sauce and the delicate strands of squash. If you are unfamiliar with this vegetable, you'll find it is a light, colorful substitute for pasta.

In a large steamer, cook the two halves of the squash, skin side up, for 15 minutes, or until soft. Let cool and, using a fork, scrape the fiber out of the vegetable skin. The strands should resemble spaghetti. Reserve.

In a large skillet over high heat, add the oil and sauté the mushrooms and garlic for about 2 minutes. Add some salt so the mushrooms release some liquid. When they get some color, add the peas, tomato sauce, and vegetable stock, always stirring with a wooden spoon. Cook over medium heat for 15 minutes, or until the sauce reduces and becomes thick. At this point correct the seasoning by adding pepper to taste and add the oregano. Add the squash and stir gently. Serve immediately.

2 pounds spaghetti squash, halved lengthwise and seeded

2 tablespoons olive oil

2 cups quartered cremini mushrooms

3 garlic cloves, minced

Salt

1 cup fresh peas

8 ounces organic tomato sauce

2 cups Vegetable Stock (page 167)

Pepper

3 tablespoons minced oregano

STUFFED YELLOW SQUASH 4 SERVINGS

I like to stuff whole vegetables for their visual appeal. These squash are as appetizing to the eye as they are to the stomach.

2 yellow squash

2 tablespoons olive oil

½ medium red onion, chopped

2 garlic cloves, minced

1 cup diced cremini mushrooms

2 plum tomatoes, diced

¼ cup white wine

3 tablespoons minced oregano

3 tablespoons minced chives

Salt and pepper

2 tablespoons grated Parmigiano-Reggiano cheese

Preheat the oven to 350°F.

Cut the squash in half lengthwise and scoop out all the pulp. Dice the pulp and reserve. Steam the halves for about 5 minutes, or until just cooked through but still firm. Reserve.

In a large skillet over high heat, add the olive oil and sauté the onion for 3 minutes, or until translucent. Add the garlic and sauté for 2 minutes more. Add the mushrooms and sauté for 5 minutes, or until soft. Then add the tomatoes and sauté for 2 minutes more, or until they're softened. Add the white wine and cook for 2 minutes more to moisten the mixture. Add the herbs and season to taste with salt and pepper. Turn the heat off and mix well.

Arrange the steamed squash in a baking dish. Divide the sautéed vegetables among the 4 squash halves and sprinkle the grated cheese on top. Bake for 10 minutes and serve.

VEGETABLE STEW 4 SERVINGS

Serve this stew as you might serve ratatouille. It's a healthy side dish for winter meals.

In a large nonstick skillet over medium heat, heat the oil and sauté the onion for 3 minutes, or until it turns translucent. Add the garlic, sweet potato, mushrooms, and zucchini and sauté for 5 minutes, or until just cooked through.

Add the wine and stock and simmer until the liquid is reduced by half, about 5 minutes.

Stir in the paprika, tomato sauce, and thyme and cook for 5 minutes more. Season to taste with salt and pepper. Right before serving, add the parsley.

2 tablespoons olive oil

½ medium Spanish onion, chopped

2 garlic cloves, minced

1 large sweet potato, cut into ½-inch cubes

2 cups quartered white mushrooms

1 large zucchini, cut in half lengthwise, then into ½-inch slices

½ cup white wine

1 cup Vegetable Stock (page 167)

½ tablespoon hot paprika

2 cups Tomato Sauce (page 166)

1 tablespoon minced thyme leaves

Salt and pepper

½ cup minced parsley

SWEET POTATO PURÉE 4 SERVINGS

When I first made this recipe, it had a full stick of butter and 2 cups of cream. Over the years, I learned how to adjust the fat content without sacrificing the voluptuous creaminess of the purée. It's a perfect match with traditional roast turkey.

In a large saucepan of boiling water, boil the sweet potatoes and carrots for about 15 minutes, or until tender.

Drain and purée them well in a food processor, adding the milk little by little, and then the margarine. Season to taste with salt.

Transfer the purée back to the saucepan and keep warm over low heat until you serve it. If the consistency is too liquid, cook a little longer, or add more milk if it's too dry.

2 sweet potatoes, peeled and cut into chunks

2 large carrots, peeled and cut into chunks

2 cups skim milk or soy milk

1 tablespoon soy margarine

Salt

WILD RICE–STUFFED TOMATOES 4 SERVINGS

Choose tomatoes that are flat on the bottom, and find pretty ones, since they're served whole in this dish. Farmers' markets are worth exploring; you can find a number of heirloom varieties in an assortment of colors.

4 large tomatoes

1 tablespoon olive oil

2 tablespoons minced fresh oregano

2 cups cooked wild rice (page 56)

Salt

Preheat the oven to 350°F.

Cut the stems off the tomatoes and scoop out the flesh and discard. In a baking dish brushed with olive oil, arrange the tomatoes. Reseason the wild rice with salt to taste before stuffing. Fill each tomato with ¼ tablespoon fresh oregano and ¼ cup of the prepared wild rice. Bake for 5 minutes and serve immediately.

VEGETABLE SPAGHETTI 4 SERVINGS

While the slicing involved in this recipe is a little time consuming, the colorful outcome makes the effort worthwhile for special meals.

2 tablespoons olive oil

½ Vidalia onion, minced

2 garlic cloves, minced

1 zucchini, sliced lengthwise ¼ inch thick, then julienned

1 yellow squash, sliced lengthwise ¼ inch thick, then julienned

1 carrot, peeled, sliced lengthwise ¼ inch thick, then julienned

1 long sweet red pepper, sliced lengthwise ¼ inch thick, then julienned

¼ cup tomato sauce

¼ cup white wine

2 tablespoons minced parsley

2 tablespoons minced oregano

Salt and pepper

In a large skillet over medium-high heat, heat the oil and sauté the onion and garlic for 2 minutes, or until the onion is translucent. Add the vegetables and cook them for another 2 to 3 minutes, or until just cooked through. Add the tomato sauce and the wine and cook for 5 minutes more to incorporate the flavors. Add the herbs and season to taste with salt and pepper. Serve immediately.

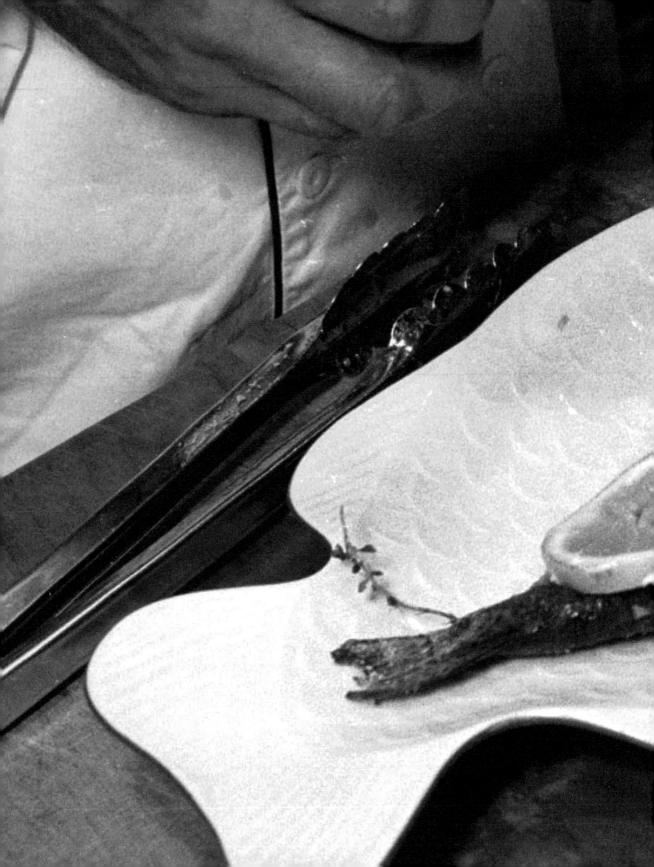

FISH, SHELLFISH, AND POULTRY

I'll be honest; I like the flavor of red meat. The thing is, my mood is better when I don't have it—it even affects my sleep patterns negatively. That aside, red meat gets pretty bad press as it is, so it's worthwhile to cut down on it as much as possible. You won't miss it so much if you can work these fish and chicken recipes into your diet; you may even notice you feel better too. Find a trustworthy fishmonger, and buy free-range, organic-fed chicken (avoid those hormones!).

CHINESE-STYLE STEAMED RED SNAPPER 4 SERVINGS

This is an authentic Chinese recipe, with julienned ginger and scallions. Just five minutes on the steamer and a quick singe with a little hot oil, and you're done.

Prepare a steamer. Season the fish chunks with salt and pepper and steam them for 5 minutes, or until tender. Transfer the fish to a serving plate and top with the scallions and ginger.

While cooking the fish, heat the oil and lime juice in separate small pans. Pour both the hot lime juice and the hot sunflower oil over the cooked fish and serve immediately.

Two 12-ounce red snapper fillets, cleaned, skin left on, and each fillet cut into 6 pieces

Salt and pepper

12 scallion stalks, sliced at a very sharp angle on the bias into pieces about 2 inches long

¼ cup julienned ginger, cut into 2-inch segments

¼ cup sunflower oil

Juice of 1 lime

H... ...INBOW TROUT 6 SERVINGS

This recipe is ... ...ple it's almost primitive. The basic technique is to stuff the fish with herbs, bake, and serve.

2 rainbow trout, cleaned, fins removed, heads and tails left on

1 teaspoon salt

1 teaspoon pepper

2 shallots, minced

2 garlic cloves, minced

¼ cup minced parsley

¼ cup olive oil

½ cup white wine

1 bunch of marjoram

1 bunch of thyme

1 lemon, thinly sliced

Preheat the oven to 450°F.

Rinse the trout and pat them dry. Cut shallow slashes into the skin of the fish on an angle, with each slash about an inch apart. Rub ½ teaspoon salt and ½ teaspoon pepper into the slashes and place the fish together in a shallow baking dish. Reserve.

In a bowl, prepare the marinade by combining the shallots, garlic, parsley, olive oil, white wine, and the remaining salt and pepper. Using a spoon, spread the marinade over the outside of the fish and into the cuts in the skin. Stuff the bellies of the fish with the marjoram, thyme, and lemon slices.

Cook on the top shelf of the oven for 15 minutes, until golden brown and crispy.

Transfer to a serving plate with a bed of greens and arrange the cooked lemon slices on top of the fish; discard the herbs.

SEARED SEA BASS 4 SERVINGS

This is an impressive dish. The combination of flavors is fantastic. Pungent and sweet, yet with a lot of personality, the sauce that dresses this fish will make you new friends and make the old ones even closer. This is great for a summer dinner, accompanied with steamed rice and vegetables.

¼ cup corn oil

One 1½-pound piece Chilean sea bass

2 shallots, minced

¼ cup shredded ginger, with juice

4 garlic cloves, minced

½ cup finely diced red bell pepper

¼ cup finely diced jalapeño or serrano pepper

¼ cup gin

1 cup Fish Stock (page 163)

3 tablespoons balsamic vinegar

3 tablespoons soy sauce

½ cup coarsely ground unsalted roasted peanuts

½ cup coarsely chopped cilantro

3 scallion stalks, sliced

In a large skillet over high heat, heat the oil. When it is very hot, sear the fish for 3 minutes on each side. Reserve on a plate. Drain all the excess oil from the pan.

Add the shallots, ginger, garlic, and peppers and sauté for 2 minutes, or until cooked through but not brown. Add the gin, fish stock, balsamic vinegar, and soy sauce and sauté for 2 to 3 minutes to blend all the flavors.

Bring the fish back to the pan and cook for 7 minutes. Using a fish spatula, which is long and wide enough do hold the whole fish, transfer the fish and sauce to a serving plate. Arrange the peanuts, cilantro, and scallions around and on top of the fish.

SEARED SCALLOPS WITH SCAMPI SAUCE 4 SERVINGS

This dish is usually made with shrimp, but I prefer the moist, soft texture and buttery taste of scallops.

Season the scallops with 1 tablespoon of the oil and salt and pepper to taste. Reserve.

In a skillet over high heat, sear the seasoned scallops for 2 minutes on each side. Remove them from the skillet and reserve.

Lower the heat to medium and add the remaining 4 tablespoons of olive oil. Add the onion and garlic and sauté for 3 minutes, or until the onion is translucent. Add salt and pepper to taste and then the scallops. Shake the pan to incorporate all together and stir in the lime juice and parsley. Serve immediately.

20 large sea scallops

5 tablespoons olive oil

Salt and pepper

1 small red onion, chopped

4 garlic cloves, minced

Juice of 1 lime

1 bunch of parsley, minced

PISTACHIO-CRUSTED SEA BASS 4 SERVINGS

The firm yet moist sea bass is balanced beautifully with the tangy, crisp crust in this recipe.

Preheat the oven to 450°F.

Brush 1 tablespoon of the olive oil onto the 4 sea bass steaks. Sprinkle on salt and pepper to taste. Reserve.

In a bowl, mix together the pistachios, mustard, lemon zest, shallot, garlic, and cilantro. Add the remaining tablespoon of olive oil and mix into a paste.

Spread the paste evenly on top of the fish steaks. Place them in a shallow baking dish and bake for 12 minutes. Serve immediately.

2 tablespoons olive oil

Four 4-ounce sea bass steaks

Salt and pepper

½ cup finely chopped pistachio nuts

2 tablespoons coarse Dijon mustard

1 tablespoon grated lemon zest

1 shallot, minced

1 garlic clove, minced

¼ cup minced cilantro

AHI POKE (TUNA WITH MANGO SALSA) 4 SERVINGS

Poke (pō-kee) is a dish that comes from Hawaii, where it is served as an appetizer or first course. Some common ingredients in poke recipes are soy sauce, scallions, and seaweed. This recipe calls for hijiki, a very tasty seaweed that complements the yellowfin tuna well. I would serve it as an entrée for a summer dinner or for lunch, accompanied by a salad.

½ cup hijiki seaweed

2 cups warm water

12 ounces yellowfin tuna (ahi), cut into 1-inch cubes

½ tablespoon red pepper flakes

1 shallot, chopped

1 tablespoon sesame seeds

2 tablespoons toasted sesame oil

1 tablespoon shoyu (soy sauce)

1 tablespoon minced parsley

½ cup coarsely ground roasted cashews

½ cup sliced scallions

1 cup mango, peeled, pitted, and diced small

Prepare a steamer.

Soak the seaweed in the warm water for 10 minutes. Drain and reserve.

Steam the tuna for 3 minutes, or until medium rare. Reserve.

In a bowl, mix together the seaweed, tuna, pepper, shallot, sesame seeds, sesame oil, shoyu, and parsley. Add the cashews, scallions, and mango right before serving so that they are crisp. Serve at room temperature.

GRILLED MARINATED SALMON 4 SERVINGS

You may be surprised by the combination of flavors in this marinade, but mostly because of how great it tastes. The soy adds a lot of flavor, while the maple syrup helps achieve a nice crust as the sugars caramelize on the grill.

Preheat the grill to a very high heat.

Rinse the salmon steaks and pat them dry.

In a shallow bowl large enough to fit the fish steaks, whisk together all the other ingredients. Marinate the salmon for 15 to 30 minutes, turning them from time to time to coat both sides.

Grill the fish for 5 minutes on each side, or until crisp on the outside. The caramelization of the marinade will brown the skin. Serve immediately.

Four 4-ounce salmon steaks, skin left on

½ cup soy sauce

2 tablespoons minced ginger

¼ cup maple syrup

½ tablespoon paprika

1 tablespoon minced thyme leaves

ORANGE ROUGHY WITH HERBED TOMATO SAUCE 4 SERVINGS

This recipe is an homage to the flavors of the Mediterranean. Orange roughy can be difficult to find, so if you can't get your hands on it, substitute sea bass.

2 tablespoons olive oil

1 yellow onion, chopped

2 garlic cloves, minced

6 plum tomatoes, seeded and diced

Salt and pepper

Juice of 1 lemon

Four 4-ounce fillets of orange roughy

¼ cup chopped parsley

¼ cup chopped basil

¼ cup chopped thyme leaves

Preheat the oven to 450°F.

In a large saucepan over high heat, add the olive oil and sauté the onion and garlic for 5 minutes, or until golden brown. Reduce the heat to medium, add the tomatoes, and simmer for 10 minutes, or until the flesh is soft and broken down. Season with salt and pepper to taste, add the lemon juice, and simmer for 2 minutes more.

Place the fish fillets in a shallow baking dish and spread the tomato sauce evenly on top of the fish. Bake for 10 minutes, or until tender. Sprinkle on the parsley, basil, and thyme leaves and serve.

SALMON IN PARCHMENT, FIVE WAYS 4 SERVINGS

I like this technique because all the flavors are steamed inside the bag, and when it is finally opened tableside your guests are treated to all the aromas. Instead of parchment you can use aluminum foil, a paper bag brushed with oil, or even a banana leaf. Just leave a little air around the fish when you seal the edges. Feel free to substitute other flavorings or other kinds of fish.

The steps for the five variations are identical.

THAI

Four 4-ounce salmon steaks
  Salt and pepper
 4 teaspoons vegetable oil
 ½ cup diced mango
 2 tablespoons minced lemongrass
 ½ cup scallions, thinly sliced on the bias

Preheat the oven to 400°F.

Rinse the salmon steaks and pat them dry. Season with salt and pepper to taste. Drizzle the oil on the steaks and reserve.

Cut parchment paper (one for each salmon steak) in circular shapes about 12 inches in diameter, fold in half, and place the fish steaks at the center of the half circle. Top with the remaining ingredients. Fold the other half of the parchment over the ingredients and crimp the edges to seal.

Place the parchment "bags" on a baking sheet and bake for 12 minutes. Serve immediately.

MEDITERRANEAN

Four 4-ounce salmon steaks
  Salt and pepper
 4 teaspoons olive oil
 2 plum tomatoes, seeded and diced
 12 black olives, pitted and chopped
 4 basil leaves, chopped

ITALIAN

Four 4-ounce salmon steaks
  Salt and pepper
 4 teaspoons olive oil
 1 medium red pepper, julienned into
    2-inch-long pieces
 2 garlic cloves, thinly sliced, 8 slices
    per clove
 ¼ cup chopped fresh oregano

ORIENTAL

Four 4-ounce salmon steaks
  Salt and pepper
 4 teaspoons sesame oil
 4 asparagus stalks, cut into
    1½-inch segments
 1 tablespoon black sesame seeds

 1 tablespoon minced ginger

HAWAIIAN

Four 4-ounce salmon steaks
  Salt and pepper
 4 teaspoons canola oil
 2 cored pineapple slices, diced
 1 shallot, minced
 2 tablespoons minced cilantro

ROAST CHICKEN WITH VEGETABLES 4 SERVINGS

Depending on the season, I use different vegetables in this recipe. In the fall I sometimes use sweet potatoes instead of red, and in late summer I sometimes add steamed corn at the end. The seasonings remain the same.

One 4- to 5-pound chicken

Salt and pepper

8 medium red potatoes, quartered, skin on

4 tablespoons olive oil

½ cup white wine

2 yellow peppers, seeded, de-ribbed, and cut into bite-size chunks

2 cups quartered button mushrooms

4 shallots, peeled and halved

7 or 8 garlic cloves, crushed

Juice of 1 lime

1 bunch of parsley

10 sage leaves, minced

Leaves from 10 oregano sprigs, minced

Preheat the oven to 400°F.

Rinse the chicken and pat dry. Rub with salt and pepper to taste. Place the chicken with the potatoes on a baking pan, drizzle on 2 tablespoons of the olive oil and ¼ cup white wine, and bake on the bottom oven rack for about 20 minutes.

In a bowl, combine the peppers, mushrooms, shallots, and garlic and season with the remaining 2 tablespoons olive oil, the lime juice, the remaining ¼ cup white wine, the parsley, and salt and pepper to taste. Toss well to combine all the flavors. Add to the roasting pan with the chicken and potatoes.

Cook for 20 minutes more. Add the sage and oregano, mixing them gently with all the ingredients in the roasting pan. Roast, uncovered, until the chicken is done and the juices run clear when the thigh is pricked with a skewer (about 10 to 15 minutes more). Serve hot.

ROAST CHICKEN STUFFED WITH HERBED PISTACHIO GREMOLATA 4 SERVINGS

The gremolata is stuffed under the skin, so the flavors are concentrated and infused into the meat.

Preheat the oven to 400°F.

Rinse the chicken and pat dry. Gently slide your fingers under the skin to loosen it from the meat of the breasts, legs, and back. Try not to break the skin.

To make the gremolata, in a food processor, put the shallots, 4 of the minced garlic cloves, the oregano, chives, pistachios, parsley, 2 tablespoons of the olive oil, the lime juice, mustard, and salt and pepper to taste. Pulse until the mixture achieves the consistency of bread crumbs.

Little by little, carefully stuff all the gremolata under the chicken's skin.

In a skillet over medium heat, add the remaining 2 tablespoons of olive oil and brown the remaining minced garlic clove. Reserve.

Place the chicken in a roasting pan and roast on the lower rack of the oven for about 50 minutes, or until the juices run clear when the thigh is pricked with a skewer. Brush the garlic-flavored oil onto the chicken two or three times while it roasts. Remove from the oven, let rest for 10 minutes, and serve.

One 4-pound roasting chicken

2 shallots, minced

5 garlic cloves, minced

1 bunch of oregano, leaves minced

1 bunch of chives, minced

½ cup ground pistachios

1 bunch of parsley, minced

4 tablespoons olive oil

Juice of 1 lime

1 tablespoon Dijon mustard

Salt and pepper

SALT-CRUSTED CHICKEN 4 SERVINGS

Before you think this recipe sounds crazy, let me tell you this method not only gives you a crisp crust, but very moist meat. The salt simply encases the chicken, without overseasoning. To top it off, the presentation is immensely dramatic. Bring the mysterious white mound to the table and crack the crust open for your guests.

2 bay leaves

2 rosemary sprigs

1 shallot, coarsely chopped

2 garlic cloves, crushed

One 4½-pound roasting chicken

5 pounds coarse sea salt

4 egg whites, beaten

Preheat the oven to 400°F.

Select a deep baking dish that fits the chicken tightly, and line it with a double layer of heavy foil. The foil should hang over the top edge of the baking dish.

Place the bay leaves, rosemary, shallot, and garlic on a piece of cheesecloth and tie with kitchen string to create a cheesecloth bag.

Stuff the chicken cavity with the bag and, using kitchen string, truss the chicken neatly so the salt will stay out.

Make a nest of salt on the foil in the baking dish, place the chicken inside, and cover the chicken with salt, encasing it completely. Using a spatula, spread the beaten egg whites over the top of the salt to seal. Cover with the overhanging foil and bake for 2 hours.

Take the foil out of the baking dish and unwrap the foil package. (Take the chicken to the table at this point if you want drama!) Crack open the salt crust and brush away any salt residue. Cut and remove the kitchen string and the seasoning bag before carving.

CURRIED CHICKEN STEW 4 TO 6 SERVINGS

I cook a lot of chicken. In my search for different ways to cook it, I began experimenting with techniques from India. This recipe is aromatic and imparts a richness without actually being heavy. I would even cook this without the chicken; the leftover potatoes are fantastic.

In a large skillet over high heat, add the olive oil and sauté the chicken until it is well browned, about 5 minutes.

Add the potatoes and cook for 3 minutes, stirring them with a wooden spoon. Add the shallots, garlic, and carrot and cook for 3 minutes more, until the shallots are translucent. Add the nutmeg, cinnamon, and curry powder and cook for 1 minute, always stirring to mix up all the flavors added to the pan.

Add the tomatoes, wine, chicken stock, bay leaves, and green beans. Reduce the heat to medium-low and simmer, uncovered, for 30 minutes, or until the sauce reduces by half and the potatoes are tender.

Discard the bay leaves, add the parsley, and season with salt and pepper to taste. Serve hot.

3 tablespoons olive oil

¾ pound chicken, dark and white meat, cut into bite-size chunks

4 medium russet potatoes, peeled and cut into 1-inch cubes

2 shallots, chopped

4 garlic cloves, chopped

1 large carrot, quartered lengthwise and cut into 1-inch segments

1 teaspoon grated nutmeg

1 teaspoon ground cinnamon

1 tablespoon curry powder

4 plum tomatoes, seeded and coarsely chopped

1 cup dry white wine

2½ cups Chicken Stock (page 162)

3 bay leaves

2 cups green beans, cut into 1-inch segments

¼ cup minced parsley

Salt and pepper

CHICKEN CACCIATORE 4 SERVINGS

I prefer to cook this Italian-American stew with boneless chicken. The fresh, cooked tomatoes are delicious.

2 tablespoons olive oil

1 pound skinless, boneless dark and/or white chicken meat, cut into bite-size chunks

1 medium Spanish onion, coarsely chopped

2 garlic cloves, minced

1 green bell pepper, cored, seeded, and cut into bite-size chunks

1 red bell pepper, cored, seeded, and cut into bite-size chunks

2 cups quartered white mushrooms

½ cup dry white wine

1½ cups Chicken Stock (page 162)

4 cups coarsely chopped plum tomatoes

Salt and pepper

¼ cup chopped fresh oregano

Red pepper flakes

In a large skillet over high heat, add the oil and sauté the chicken on all sides until well browned, about 5 minutes.

Add the onion, garlic, peppers, and mushrooms and sauté for 5 minutes, shaking the pan to cook all the ingredients evenly, until the onion is translucent and the peppers and mushrooms are just cooked through.

Add the wine and deglaze the pan (see page 4), using a wooden spoon, then stir in the chicken stock and tomatoes. Bring to a boil.

Add salt and pepper to taste, the oregano, and red pepper flakes to taste, then lower the heat and simmer for 20 minutes, or until the sauce has reduced and thickened. Serve hot.

GRILLED CHICKEN 4 SERVINGS

I have a special technique for keeping grilled chicken juicy. I marinate it, leave it on the bone, and leave the skin on until there's about ten minutes left of cooking time. By taking the skin off at that moment, you eliminate a lot of the fat but have allowed the meat to be basted and protected from the flames. With turning, the chicken still achieves a nice color for serving.

Preheat the grill.

In a large bowl, combine all the marinade ingredients. Add the chicken breasts, cover with plastic wrap, and refrigerate for at least 30 minutes.

Place the chicken on the hot grill and turn every 3 minutes. Every time you turn the breasts, brush on the marinade. After 15 minutes, remove the skin and brush the marinade on the skinless breasts. Grill 10 minutes more, continuing to turn every 3 minutes. (During the final 10 minutes, discontinue brushing on the marinade to avoid salmonella poisoning.) Serve immediately.

MARINADE

1 cup finely diced sweet pineapple

2 shallots, chopped

4 garlic cloves, minced

2 tablespoons minced ginger

1 bunch of basil, leaves minced

1 cup white wine

1 cup balsamic vinegar

½ cup soy sauce

1 cup warm water

4 chicken breast halves, with the bone and skin

GRILLED TURKEY TENDERLOINS 4 SERVINGS

I love pork. It's true. Happily, turkey tenderloins look similar to pork tenderloins and end up tasting very similar as well. Turkey tenderloins are not easy to find, but they are a delicacy and well worth the trouble.

MARINADE

1 cup balsamic vinegar

1 cup white wine

½ cup soy sauce

2 tablespoons minced ginger

2 tablespoons minced shallots

2 garlic cloves, minced

1 cup chopped pineapple

¼ cup minced basil

Salt and pepper to taste

2 turkey tenderloins

Preheat the grill to high.

In a large bowl, mix the marinade ingredients. Add the tenderloins and marinate for 30 minutes.

Place the tenderloins on the hot grill and cook them about 5 minutes on each side, or until cooked through. Cut the tenderloins in medallions about 1 inch thick and serve.

WEEKEND RECIPES

A little heavier on time and calories, these recipes are meant to be lingered over, both in their preparation and their eating. Several of them are my own family recipes, full of nostalgia and good memories. So, satisfy the basic pleasure of feeding people this weekend; invite a crowd—they'll all end up in the kitchen anyway.

THAI CHICKEN CUPS 10 SERVINGS

Oodles of Noodles, a Thai restaurant in Hawaii, makes a version of this recipe with duck. I re-created it at home with chicken. It's got everything—it's sweet and sour and crunchy. I serve it as an appetizer or over a bed of salad greens for lunch.

In a small saucepan over high heat, heat the oil. Test the oil temperature by dipping in 1 wonton skin. If it bubbles quickly, the oil is ready for frying. Drape a wonton skin on the outside of a ladle cup (about 2 inches in diameter) and dip it in the hot oil (see illustration). Fry it quickly, on the ladle, until just browned, or about 30 seconds. Repeat with the remaining wontons. Dry the cups on paper towels and reserve.

In a medium bowl, season the chicken thighs with salt and pepper to taste. Add the olive oil and mix well to coat the chicken. Place the chicken in a large skillet over medium heat and sauté until dark brown, about 10 minutes. Add the garlic after 5 minutes. Let cool, then dice the meat.

In a large bowl, mix the green cabbage, red cabbage, cilantro, peanuts, Thai pepper, plum sauce, and diced chicken. Refrigerate for 20 minutes.

To serve, scoop some of the cabbage mixture into each wonton cup and arrange the cups on a serving plate. If you like, surround the cups with salad greens.

2 cups vegetable oil

10 square wonton skins

2 skinless, boneless chicken thighs, trimmed of fat

Salt and pepper

1 tablespoon olive oil

3 garlic cloves, minced

1 cup thinly sliced green cabbage

1 cup thinly sliced red cabbage

1 cup minced cilantro

½ cup coarsely ground roasted peanuts

1 ground dried Thai pepper

1 cup Plum Sauce (recipe follows)

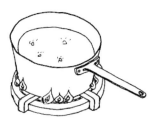

PLUM SAUCE MAKES 1 CUP

In a saucepan over medium heat, cook ½ cup water, the brown sugar, and the plums for about 20 minutes, or until a nice sauce consistency is reached. Let cool and pureé in a blender.

½ cup packed brown sugar

2 plums, pitted, skin on

BIG SALAD WITH SHRIMP 8 TO 10 SERVINGS

Does the title scare you? Don't worry, there's a whole meal in this recipe. I serve it in the summertime by the pool.

Preheat the grill to high.

In a large bowl, combine all the ingredients for the vegetable marinade. Add the vegetables and marinate for 30 minutes. In another bowl, combine all the ingredients for the shrimp marinade. Marinate the shrimp for 15 minutes.

Grill the vegetables for 10 minutes, or until tender, turning once. Pay attention to the scallions and asparagus, as they will cook faster than the other vegetables. Reserve.

Grill the shrimp, turning once, until they are pink but still tender, or about 1 to 2 minutes on each side. Reserve.

In a salad spinner, wash the lettuces. Dry well. On a large serving plate, arrange the greens, then the mango slices and quartered tomatoes in a decorative style. Top with the grilled vegetables and shrimp.

Prepare the topping: In a skillet over high heat, add the olive oil and sauté the minced garlic for 3 minutes. Add the pine nuts and sauté until they start to brown, about 1 to 2 minutes. Pour the topping onto the vegetables and shrimp. Serve immediately with the Blueberry and Balsamic Dressing.

MARINADE FOR VEGETABLES

½ cup balsamic vinegar

½ cup soy sauce

½ cup white wine

Juice of 1 lime

2 tablespoons olive oil

½ Spanish onion, sliced

3 garlic cloves, minced

3 tablespoons minced ginger

10 thyme sprigs, leaves minced

Salt and pepper

VEGETABLES

1 large red bell pepper, thickly sliced

1 large yellow pepper, thickly sliced

2 large portobello mushrooms, thickly sliced

6 asparagus stalks, halved

6 scallions

MARINADE FOR SHRIMP

2 tablespoons olive oil

Juice of 1 lime

1 tablespoon Dijon mustard

1 shallot, minced

2 garlic cloves, minced

¼ cup minced parsley

Salt and pepper to taste

2 ounces large shrimp, cleaned and deveined

SALAD

2 heads of Boston lettuce, torn into bite-size pieces

2 cups baby arugula

2 cups baby spinach

1 head of radicchio, torn into bite-size pieces

1 large mango, peeled and sliced

6 plum tomatoes, quartered

TOPPING

¼ cup olive oil

4 garlic cloves, minced

¼ cup pine nuts

Blueberry and Balsamic Dressing (page 65)

MARINATED ROAST TURKEY 12 SERVINGS

This recipe is for weekends, so I won't include the traditional stuffing, sweet potatoes, gravy, and cranberry sauce with it. However, the marinade is so good that you'll probably want to use it again for your Thanksgiving dinner. Note that you'll need to marinate the turkey the day before you roast it.

Rinse the turkey well and pat it dry. Place it into a bowl, pan, or container big enough to fit the turkey. Add all the remaining ingredients and a gallon of water and marinate, covered and in the refrigerator, for at least 24 hours, turning the turkey several times so that it marinates evenly.

Preheat the oven to 250°F. Transfer the turkey to a roasting pan fitted with a rack. With a slotted spoon, scoop out 2 to 3 cups of the solid ingredients from the marinade and stuff them into the turkey. Cover with aluminum foil and roast for about 2 hours. Uncover the turkey and turn the heat up to 350°F. Roast for 2 hours more, basting occasionally with the marinade, until the juices run clear when the thigh is pricked with a skewer. Remove the turkey and let it sit for 10 minutes before carving.

One 12- to 15-pound turkey

1 large Spanish onion, minced

15 garlic cloves, minced

¼ cup minced ginger

2 cups diced sweet pineapple

1 small green papaya, diced

5 rosemary sprigs, leaves only, minced

1 cup minced sage

1 cup minced parsley

1 cup minced chives

1 bottle dry white wine

1 cup balsamic vinegar

1 cup soy sauce

Salt and pepper to taste

XIMXIM (CHICKEN AND SHRIMP STEW) 8 TO 10 SERVINGS

This is a very traditional stew from Bahia in northeast Brazil. I am in love with my version of this recipe, especially because I succeeded in taking out the coconut milk and substituting soy milk and grated coconut. It goes beautifully with Rice Pilaf (page 137), which balances the heat.

In a small bowl, combine the lime juice, white wine, and olive oil. Place the shrimp and chicken in two separate bowls and season both to taste with salt and pepper. Divide the marinade between them and marinate for 30 minutes.

Drain the shrimp and chicken, reserving the marinade for later use. In a very large skillet or a large saucepan over high heat, sauté the shrimp until they are pink, about 3 minutes, or until just cooked through. Reserve the shrimp.

In the same pan, sauté the chicken until golden brown, about 10 minutes. Remove the chicken and reserve.

MARINADE

Juice of 1 lime

½ cup white wine

2 tablespoons olive oil

2 pounds medium shrimp, peeled and deveined

4 chicken breasts, skinned and cut into 1-inch cubes

4 boneless chicken thighs, skinned, fat trimmed, and cut into chunks

Salt and pepper

1 green bell pepper, diced

6 tomatoes, seeded and diced

1 cup Chicken Stock (page 162)

SAUCE

¼ cup olive oil

3 shallots, chopped

6 garlic cloves, minced

2 tablespoons minced ginger

1 cup grated coconut

½ cup ground dried shrimp (see Note)

1 dried Thai pepper, minced, with seeds, or 1 jalapeño with seeds

¼ cup ground unsalted roasted cashews

¼ cup ground unsalted roasted peanuts

1 cup chopped cilantro

1 tablespoon hot paprika

2 cups soy milk

Salt and pepper to taste

Reduce the heat to medium and add the saved marinade from both the shrimp and chicken. Stir in the green pepper, tomatoes, and chicken stock. Bring the chicken back to the pan and simmer for 20 minutes.

To make the sauce, in another skillet over high heat, add the olive oil and sauté the shallots, garlic, and ginger for 4 minutes, or until the shallots are translucent. Reduce the heat to medium and mix in all the other sauce ingredients.

Transfer the sauce to the pan with the chicken. Simmer for 10 minutes and cook until the sauce thickens. Add more salt and pepper if necessary. Add the reserved shrimp. Serve over simple basmati rice or rice pilaf.

NOTE: Dried shrimp is found in any market that sells Chinese cooking ingredients.

RICE PILAF 12 SERVINGS

We eat rice and beans in Brazil every day, with anything. The first thing my daughter learned to cook was rice. It comes so naturally that I can barely think of it as a recipe. Since white rice has none of the fiber of brown rice, but all the carbohydrates, I make this recipe only on the weekend.

¼ cup vegetable oil

2 shallots, minced

3 tablespoons minced ginger

3 garlic cloves, minced

3 cups long-grain basmati rice

Salt

6 cups boiling water

In a saucepan over medium heat, add the oil and sauté the shallots, ginger, and garlic until lightly browned, about 3 minutes. Add the rice and stir with a wooden spoon for about 2 minutes to coat all the grains with the flavor from the pan. Season to taste with salt.

Add the boiling water, cover, reduce the heat to low, and cook for 15 minutes. Turn the heat off and let it rest, covered, for about 10 minutes before serving.

FAROFA 10 SERVINGS

Farofa is derived from Brazilian native Indian cuisine. You might see this dish and think, "This just looks like flour or fine bread crumbs," but think of it as you might turkey stuffing. It is very well seasoned and becomes the perfect accompaniment with a wide range of meats and dishes. Some Brazilians eat it with bananas or scrambled eggs. I particularly like it with rice.

Peel and finely grate the yuccas, using the smallest teeth on a four-sided grater. Spread the yucca on a baking sheet and let it rest, uncovered, for 30 minutes. Preheat the oven to 200°F.

Bake the yucca for 30 minutes, stirring from time to time so it dries evenly.

In a food processor, finely grind the dried yucca to a flourlike consistency. Raise the oven temperature to 350°F. Spread the yucca on the baking sheet again and bake for only 12 minutes, or until the yucca is lightly toasted. Reserve.

In a large skillet over medium heat, add the olive oil and sauté the shallot, garlic, celery, carrot, olives, and raisins for about 5 minutes, or until the celery is softened. Add the reserved yucca "flour" and mix well. Stir in the parsley and season to taste with salt and pepper. Serve at room temperature.

2 large yuccas

¼ cup olive oil

1 shallot, minced

3 garlic cloves, minced

1 celery stalk, finely diced

1 carrot, peeled and finely diced

½ cup pitted and finely diced green olives

½ cup raisins

¼ cup minced parsley

Salt and pepper

PUDIM DE LEITE (FLAN) 8 SERVINGS

This Portuguese dessert is well worth the calories when you can spare them.

4 eggs

1 cup sweetened condensed milk

1½ cups milk

1 tablespoon cornstarch

¼ cup sugar

Preheat the oven to 350°F.

In a blender, blend the eggs, condensed milk, milk, and cornstarch. Reserve.

In a saucepan over medium heat, add the sugar and stir with a wooden spoon, just until it melts completely, about 3 to 4 minutes. Reduce the heat to low and cook until the syrup turns into a dark caramel sauce. Add 3 tablespoons water. At this point the sauce will get hard. Keep stirring until it melts again and cook to thicken the sauce a little, to the consistency of honey.

Pour the caramel sauce into a shallow baking dish big enough to hold the egg mixture as well, about 3½ cups. Tilt the dish from side to side to spread the caramel sauce and coat the dish.

Pour the egg mixture into the baking dish over the caramel sauce. Cover tightly with aluminum foil. Place the baking dish inside a larger baking dish.

Place in the oven. Fill the larger dish halfway with water. (This technique is called a "bain Marie.") Bake for 45 minutes. After that, remove the aluminum foil and bake for another 15 to 20 minutes, or until completely set. Let rest, uncovered, for about 30 minutes, or until cool. Refrigerate until ready to serve.

Run a sharp paring knife along the edge of the baking dish. Place a serving plate upside down on top of the baking dish and invert both dishes. Tap the bottom of the baking dish a few times and remove it to unmold. Refrigerate for 30 minutes. Serve cold.

PUDIM DE COCO (COCONUT PUDDING) 10 SERVINGS

My father loved this recipe. The soft pudding and crunchy coconut make for a great taste contrast, and the black prunes against the white pudding are visually appealing.

In a saucepan over low heat, heat the grated coconut and 2 tablespoons brown sugar, stirring constantly. As the sugar starts to melt, add the milk and raise the heat to medium-high. Cook until it is about to boil over, about 7 minutes. Turn off the heat and stir in the vanilla extract.

Dissolve the gelatin in ¼ cup hot water and add to the milk mixture, stirring well. Pour the mixture into a greased ring cake mold and refrigerate for at least 2 hours, or until set.

In a saucepan over medium heat, add the remaining 3 tablespoons brown sugar, 1 cup water, and the prunes. Cook for 10 minutes, then cool and refrigerate.

To serve, invert the coconut pudding onto the serving plate to unmold, arrange the prunes around the edges, and pour the prune syrup on top.

Grated white meat of 1 coconut

5 tablespoons brown sugar

1 quart milk

1 tablespoon vanilla extract

3 tablespoons unflavored gelatin

1 cup dried prunes (about 20)

ROLLED EGGPLANT 12 SERVINGS

I like to make stuffed vegetables for their presentation value. Here eggplants are rolled rather than stuffed, but they have an equally attractive effect on the plate.

Roast the peppers following the technique on page 6. Reserve.

Cut off both ends of the eggplants and discard. Slice the rest lengthwise into six to eight $1/4$-inch-thick slices per eggplant. A mandoline would make perfectly even slices, but if you don't have one, use a long-bladed knife. Discard the outside slices, since they are not long enough to make the rolls.

In a large saucepan over high heat, bring $1/2$ gallon of water to a boil. Add 1 teaspoon salt and boil the eggplant slices in small batches for about 2 minutes. You want to cook the eggplants just until tender but not too soft. Remove from the saucepan, dry on paper towels, and reserve.

In a large skillet big enough to hold all the spinach (if not, do it in two batches), add the olive oil and sauté the shallot and garlic for about 4 minutes, or until the shallot is golden brown. Add the spinach and cook, stirring with a wooden spoon, until it is all wilted, or about 3 minutes. Season to taste with salt and pepper and reserve.

2 red bell peppers, roasted and sliced

2 large, long eggplants

Salt

2 tablespoons olive oil

1 shallot, minced

2 garlic cloves, minced

1 large bunch of spinach

Pepper

¾ pound mozzarella cheese

1 cup sliced toasted almonds

¼ cup minced parsley

Cut the mozzarella into 1- × 3-inch chunks. Your aim is to have the mozzarella chunks in the center of each roll, so try to make them the same size of each eggplant slice's width. Reserve.

Start to make the rolls by building layers with the ingredients; first the eggplant slices, then some wilted spinach. Sprinkle on some toasted almonds (reserving ¼ cup for garnish); lay the roasted peppers on top and finally the mozzarella chunks. Carefully roll it up. Secure each roll with a toothpick. Transfer the rolls to a large baking dish and refrigerate for 20 minutes.

Preheat the oven to 450°F.

Bake the eggplant rolls for 5 minutes. Serve immediately, garnished with sliced toasted almonds and minced parsley.

DESSERTS

Give me some sugar, a couple sticks of butter, a dozen eggs, flour, and last but not least, some great chocolate, and I will give you a delicious dessert. How to make it healthy? Forget about it. You can use healthy ingredients as part of a great dessert recipe, but in essence, if you use even one of the ingredients mentioned above, you really can't say that it is good for your health. I was raised eating incredibly good desserts after meals. My grandmother was a great "doceira" (dessert maker), besides being a sweet lady, and my mom followed in her steps, even cooking desserts for restaurants for quite a while. Coming from this heritage didn't help me to cook healthy, but it did help me to develop my taste buds. My intention is to make these dessert recipes as healthy as possible by using fresh ingredients and limiting the use of those same ingredients I learned to love in my childhood (forgive me, Grandma), while never sacrificing flavor. Remember that moderation is the key to good health. Enjoy!

EGG WHITE FLAN 8 SERVINGS

As a lover of flan, I was amazed when I discovered this lighter recipe and actually found it delicious. Served with fruit, the presentation is beautiful.

Preheat the oven to 450°F.

In an electric mixer, add the egg whites and the salt. Whip until foamy, then add ¼ cup of the sugar, one spoon at a time while whipping, until the mixture forms soft peaks. Fold in the lemon zest and vanilla extract. Reserve.

In a saucepan over medium heat, add the remaining ¼ cup sugar and stir with a wooden spoon until it melts completely. Reduce the heat to low and cook until the syrup turns into a dark caramel sauce. Add 3 tablespoons water. At this point the sauce will get hard. Keep stirring until it melts again and cook to thicken the sauce a little, to the consistency of honey.

Take eight ¼ cup ramekins and divide the caramel sauce among them. Work quickly so that the caramel does not harden.

Fold the meringue into the caramel-coated ramekins almost to the top edge, using a rubber spatula. Bake for 5 minutes, or until golden brown. Let cool and refrigerate for at least 2 hours. To serve, run a sharp knife around the edges and invert the ramekins right onto the serving plates. Decorate with strawberries and garnish with mint leaves.

3 egg whites

Pinch of salt

½ cup sugar

Zest of 1 lemon

1 tablespoon vanilla extract

16 strawberries or other berries

16 mint leaves

BLUEBERRY TART WITH ALMOND CRUST 8 SERVINGS

This (nearly) flourless crust works great with any kind of fruit. I use blueberries here for their high nutritional and antioxidant value.

2 cups skinless slivered almonds

½ cup plus 2 tablespoons brown sugar

3 egg whites

1 egg yolk

2 tablespoons whole wheat flour, sifted

1 cup soy milk

3 tablespoons vanilla extract

Butter or light oil (to grease the pan)

1 tablespoon granulated sugar (for dusting the pan)

1 tablespoon lemon juice

1 tablespoon rum (optional)

½ tablespoon freshly grated nutmeg (optional)

3 cups blueberries

16 mint leaves (for garnish)

Preheat the oven to 350°F.

In a food processor, finely grind the almonds. Pass them through a strainer to remove the largest chunks and return the rest to the food processor. Add ½ cup of the brown sugar, the egg whites and yolk, flour, soy milk, and vanilla extract. Mix until well blended.

Grease the bottom of a 9-inch springform pan, sprinkle on some sugar, and pour the batter into it. Bake for 20 to 25 minutes, or until it browns slightly and a toothpick inserted in the center comes out clean. Cool completely and invert right onto the serving plate. Reserve.

Make the topping: In a large nonstick skillet over medium heat, add the remaining 2 tablespoons brown sugar and cook, stirring, until it starts to melt. Add the lemon juice, 3 tablespoons water, rum (if using), nutmeg, and blueberries. Reduce the heat to medium-low and cook, stirring constantly, for 5 minutes, or until warmed through. Using a slotted spoon, transfer the blueberry mixture right onto the crust. Serve warm, garnished with mint leaves.

DOCE DE ABOBORA (PUMPKIN DESSERT) 8 SERVINGS

My mother makes this dish. The pumpkin achieves a beautiful translucent orange and is intensely sweet, so the serving size is small. In Brazil, we serve this with a slightly salty, soft fresh farmer's cheese.

In a saucepan over low heat, add the pumpkin cubes and sprinkle the sugar on top. Cover and cook for about 1 hour. *Do not stir to avoid breaking up the chunks.*

Add the cloves, cinnamon, and vanilla to the pan (again, do not stir) and cook, covered, for another hour.

Let it rest, covered, for 30 minutes. Gently transfer to a serving bowl with the cinnamon and cloves and only half the syrup (discard the other half). Refrigerate for at least 30 minutes, covered with plastic wrap. Serve cold.

2 cups pumpkin, peeled, seeded, and cut into ½-inch cubes

2 cups sugar

10 whole cloves

5 cinnamon sticks, broken into pieces

2 teaspoons vanilla extract

ARROZ DOCE (RICE PUDDING) 8 SERVINGS

This is my "spa" version of rice pudding. I use brown rice, pulsing it first in a food processor to break it up and shorten the cooking time. Also, I toast the rice and melt the sugar first to heighten the flavor and sweetness of the dish to heighten.

1 cup uncooked long-grain brown rice

½ cup brown sugar

2 quarts fat-free milk

1 cup raisins

Zest of 1 lemon, cut into 1-inch-thick strips

3 cinnamon sticks, broken into pieces

2 tablespoons vanilla extract

In a food processor, coarsely grind the rice. What you want is to try to break every rice grain into two or three pieces, as it speeds up the cooking process.

In a large saucepan or stockpot over medium heat, add the rice and toast it, stirring constantly (see page 5), for a minute or two. Add the sugar and cook until it starts to melt, stirring vigorously with a wooden spoon to give the rice some of the flavor of the sugar.

Add the milk, raisins, lemon zest, and cinnamon sticks. Reduce the heat and simmer, uncovered, for about 30 minutes, stirring constantly to avoid scorching. Taste for the texture of the rice and continue to cook until you achieve the consistency you like. Add the vanilla extract, stir, and let it rest for 10 minutes.

Before transferring to serving plate(s), stir again to break up any lumps or scorching. Serve warm with the lemon zest and cinnamon sticks. If you plan on serving it later, cover with plastic wrap. To reheat, use a double boiler.

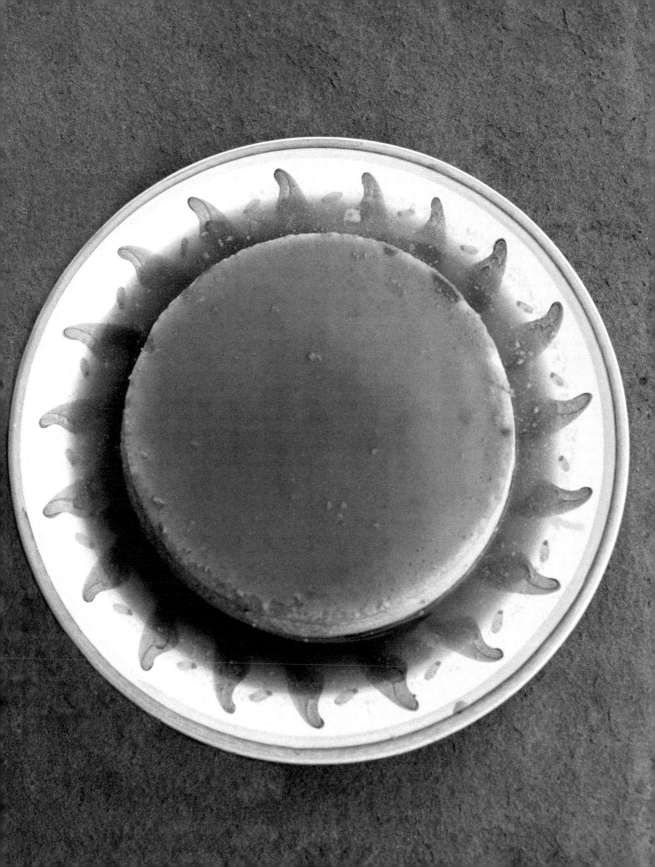

PEAR PUDDING WITH BLUEBERRY PURÉE 8 SERVINGS

The blueberry purée in this recipe is a stunning color, and the lime marries with the pear in the pudding, to make it one of my "bestsellers."

PEAR PUDDING

5 large ripe Bartlett pears

Juice of 2 limes

¼ cup sugar

2 cups finely ground and sifted almonds

3 egg whites

1 egg yolk

2 tablespoons flour, sifted

2 tablespoons vanilla extract

BLUEBERRY PURÉE

1 tablespoon sugar

1 tablespoon lime juice

1 tablespoon rum

½ tablespoon freshly grated nutmeg (optional)

1 cup blueberries

Preheat the oven to 350°F.

Peel, core, and cut the pears into chunks. Place the chunks immediately in a bowl with the lime juice to prevent browning. In a food processor, add the pears, mix well with the rest of the pear pudding ingredients, and pour into a deep baking dish. Bake for 20 to 25 minutes, or until light brown. Let cool completely and refrigerate.

In a saucepan over medium heat, add the ingredients for the blueberry purée with 3 cups water and cook until the liquid reduces by half, or about 15 minutes. Let it cool completely, then purée well in a food processor or a blender. Pour over the refrigerated pudding (in the baking dish) and serve.

DOCE DE COCO (COCONUT COOKIES) MAKES ABOUT 16 COOKIES

Much like macaroons, these little cookies are perfect with coffee at dessert or as an afternoon treat.

In an electric mixer, whip the egg white until it forms soft peaks. Reserve.

In a saucepan over medium heat, add the sugar and stir with a wooden spoon until it starts to melt. Reduce the heat and add the coconut, cinnamon, and cloves. Keep stirring until the mixture thickens, or about 3 minutes. Remove from the heat and *carefully* immerse the bottom of the saucepan in a bowl of room-temperature water to stop the cooking process.

Using a tablespoon, drop scoops of the coconut mixture onto a lightly greased baking sheet, leaving some space between the scoops because the mixture will spread as it cools. Allow some time for the mixture to set. Store in an airtight container.

1 egg white, beaten

1 cup dark brown sugar

1 cup grated fresh or packaged coconut

¼ teaspoon ground cinnamon

Pinch of ground cloves

LIGHT FLOATING ISLANDS 8 SERVINGS

I make this recipe with egg whites instead of the traditional meringue, and a vanilla sauce thickened with starch instead of the more fattening egg yolks.

3 egg whites

Pinch of salt

¼ cup plus 2 tablespoons sugar

Lemon zest

2 quarts whole milk

1 egg yolk

1 tablespoon flour

2 tablespoons vanilla extract

Preheat the oven to 200°F.

In an electric mixer, beat the egg whites with the salt. As they start to turn white, add ¼ cup of the sugar, a tablespoon at a time, and the lemon zest. Beat until the meringue forms soft peaks but is not stiff.

In a large saucepan over medium heat, stir the remaining 2 tablespoons sugar. As it starts to melt, add the milk. Reduce the heat and simmer, stirring constantly to avoid scorching, for 10 minutes.

Using a ladle, put about ¼ cup of the warm milk into a small bowl. Stir in the egg yolk and flour, whisking vigorously to avoid any lumps or cooked egg yolk. Add this mixture back to the milk in the saucepan on the stove, add the vanilla extract, and, with a wooden spoon, stir until it thickens a little. Refrigerate.

Line two cookie sheets with parchment paper. Using a tablespoon, drop scoops of the meringue gently onto the cookie sheets. Bake for 10 to 15 minutes, or until golden brown.

Pour the vanilla-milk mixture into a shallow serving bowl or plate. Using a spatula, transfer the meringues one by one to the serving plate. Serve cold.

BASIC RECIPES

The recipes in this section can be used as building blocks. Many of them are called for in other recipes in this book. Making your own stock, for example, adds a lot of flavor to more complex soups. I've also included information on how to store them for later use.

CHICKEN STOCK MAKES 1 GALLON

The consistency of this stock changes depending on the bones you use. Young chicken contains a high percentage of cartilage and other connective tissues that make the stock more gelatinous.

In a large stockpot over medium heat, add the chicken bones and sauté for 5 minutes. Add all the other ingredients with a gallon of water, bring to a boil, lower the heat, and simmer for 3 to 4 hours.

Strain the stock through a sieve (a very fine strainer) lined with cheesecloth. Let cool and store for future use. You can refrigerate the stock for up to 5 days in the refrigerator. The other option is to freeze the stock. I like to pour it into ice cube trays, then store the frozen cubes in sealed plastic bags and use as needed. You can store chicken stock this way for up to 2 months.

4 pounds chicken bones, some meat left on, cut into 3-inch lengths

1 bottle dry white wine

2 medium Spanish onions, chopped

2 carrots, peeled and chopped

4 celery stalks, chopped

½ cup chopped parsley, leaves and stems

½ cup minced thyme leaves

2 or 3 bay leaves

10 peppercorns, cracked

FISH STOCK MAKES 1 GALLON

Use bones from a lean flatfish like sole or turbot. Bones from oily fish like salmon will give the stock a very strong, fishy flavor. If you use the heads in the stock, cut away the gills.

¼ cup vegetable oil

5 to 6 pounds fish bones

1 large Spanish onion, chopped

2 leeks, white part only, chopped

1 large parsnip, peeled and chopped

2 celery stalks, chopped

1 cup chopped white mushrooms

1 bottle dry white wine

½ cup chopped parsley, leaves and stems

½ cup minced thyme leaves

2 or 3 bay leaves

10 peppercorns, cracked

In a large stockpot over high heat, add the oil, fish bones, onion, leeks, parsnip, celery, and mushrooms and sauté for 5 minutes. Add all the other ingredients with a gallon of water and bring to a boil. Reduce the heat and simmer for 40 minutes. Strain through a sieve (a very fine strainer) lined with cheesecloth. Let cool and store for future use. You can refrigerate the stock for up to 5 days in the refrigerator. The other option is to freeze the stock. I like to pour it into ice cube trays, then store the frozen cubes in sealed plastic bags and use as needed. You can store fish stock this way for up to 1 month.

TOMATO SAUCE MAKES ½ GALLON

In a wide saucepan over medium heat, add the olive oil and cook the onions and garlic until tender and slightly browned, or about 3 minutes. Add the tomatoes and either the water, chicken stock, or white wine plus your choice of herbs: oregano, parsley, and/or basil (in any combination). This means that you may use anywhere from ½ cup to 1½ cups of herbs total. Raise the heat to high and bring to a boil, then lower the heat to medium and simmer, uncovered, for 1 hour, stirring frequently to prevent scorching. Taste the sauce as it cooks and add salt and pepper to taste.

¼ cup olive oil

2 large Spanish onions, minced

4 garlic cloves, minced

5 to 6 pounds fresh plum tomatoes, chopped

2 cups water, Chicken Stock (page 162), or white wine

½ cup oregano, and/or ½ cup parsley, and/or ½ cup basil

Salt and pepper

VEGETABLE STOCK MAKES 1 GALLON

¼ cup vegetable oil

2 medium Spanish onions, chopped

4 garlic cloves, crushed

3 leeks, white part only, chopped

3 celery stalks, chopped

2 carrots, peeled and chopped

4 plum tomatoes, chopped

1 bottle dry white wine

½ cup chopped parsley, with stems

½ cup minced thyme leaves

2 or 3 bay leaves

10 peppercorns, cracked

In a large stockpot over medium heat, add the oil and sauté the onions, garlic, leeks, celery, carrots, and tomatoes for 5 minutes. Raise the heat to high, add the wine and a gallon of water, and bring to a boil. Add the rest of the ingredients, lower the heat to medium, and simmer, uncovered, for 1 hour. Let cool and store for future use. You can refrigerate the stock for up to 1 week in the refrigerator. The other option is to freeze the stock. I like to pour it into ice cube trays, then store the frozen cubes in sealed plastic bags and use as needed. You can store vegetable stock this way for up to 2 months.

MAYONNAISE MAKES 4 CUPS

In a blender or a food processor, blend the egg yolks until they start to become a thick, creamy light yellow. Add the lime juice and mix for a minute or two just to blend it in, then slowly drizzle in the vegetable oil while blending constantly. Add salt and pepper to taste. The mayonnaise will be ready when it holds soft peaks. Store it in an airtight container in the refrigerator for 1 to 2 weeks.

4 egg yolks

2 tablespoons lime juice

3 cups vegetable oil

Salt and pepper

MANGO SALSA MAKES ABOUT 5 CUPS

2 mangoes, peeled, seeded, and diced

1 large red onion, diced

8 plum tomatoes, seeded and diced

1 jalapeño pepper, minced, with seeds

1 green pepper, seeded and diced

Juice of 1 lime

¼ cup tomato juice (see Note), or the juice of 1 beefsteak tomato

½ cup minced cilantro

In a glass bowl, add all the ingredients in the order that they are listed. Mix well, cover with plastic wrap, and refrigerate for a few hours or overnight. Serve the salsa with a salad or grilled fish.

NOTE: If you don't have a juicer, use canned tomato juice, but make the effort to find a good brand and keep in mind that organic is always preferred.

POTATO STICKS MAKES 2 CUPS

2 cups vegetable oil

Salt

2 large Idaho baking potatoes or sweet potatoes, peeled and cut into 2-inch-long julienne strips

In a medium skillet over high heat, add the oil and heat for 3 minutes, or until the oil is hot enough so that a test potato strip sizzles on contact. In a large bowl, salt the potatoes to taste. (The salt will draw out some of the moisture and help the sticks to be crisp outside and tender inside.) Add the potatoes and fry until the color begins to change, but remove before they become golden. Scoop out and drain on a paper towel. Serve as a topping for salads.

Acknowledgments

This is a unique moment in my life. I have the great satisfaction of seeing a dream come true and am filled with pride and happiness. I traveled a very long way to get here and there are a few people without whom this would not have been possible.

To Michael Fuchs, my biggest and warmest thanks. Under your leadership I've found the path to a healthier lifestyle. Thank you for always giving me the freedom to experiment in the kitchen (and for being so patient with a few screwups). Through you I had the pleasure of meeting Jay Williams, who taught me so much about nutrition. It was an honor to be a (little) part of her book, *The 24-Hour Turnaround*, a serious study about health and the way to achieve it.

Others who deserve thanks include: Ellen and Bob Grimes, I admire your refined taste for good food, and thank you for always believing in my talent and for the encouraging words. Lois and Joe Block, thank you for your generosity and friendship, as well as many good times in Hawaii. Vania and Robert Plan, you are such very dear friends. Raquel Barros, my coworker, thank you for always being there for me whenever I needed help. Thanks to my mother, Inez Ratto (I love you, Mom), for a few recipes. To David Klenicki from Pond House Designs, for the fantastic kitchen he had built for me, and Francine Leof, his wife, for the oven-dried tomato recipe. Thanks to the nice people from Sgaglio's Market Place in Katonah and Mount Kisco Farm. And Bernard Kerik, a great man, and his crew: Sonny Archer, Hector Santiago, Bobby Picciano, Mike Jermyn, Craig Taylor, and Maureen Casey from the NYPD, and to Joe Kerik and Vinny Barchini. My perennial respect to all of them.

Ann Volkwein, thank you for always being focused and for keeping me going. Thank you for your talent. You are a big part of this book.

To the people from ReganBooks: Cassie Jones, Aliza Fogelson, and Dan Taylor, thank you for the fantastic work you've done. And Judith Regan, for your steadfast belief in this project and unwavering encouragement; I am forever grateful.

Finally, the women in my life: Gabriela, my loving daughter, and Caroline, my better half, thank you for always being there for me. You are my inspiration. For you, all my love.

Index

ahi poke (tuna) with mango salsa, 105

almond crust, blueberry tart with, 149

antipasto, 12

appetizers, 12-27

    antipasto, 12

    ceviche, 13

    chicken roll-ups, 25

    crabmeat-stuffed mushrooms, 14

    green grape salsa, 15

    guacamole, 16

    roasted garlic and tofu spread, 21

    salmon spread roll-ups, 18-19

    spring rolls, 27

    stuffed cherry tomatoes, 19

    tuna spread roll-ups, 20

arroz doce (rice pudding), 153

arugula, in tuna spread roll-ups, 20

asparagus and roasted red peppers, 68

avocado, 16

basic recipes, 162-71

beans, dried, 5

    black bean soup, 30

    garbanzo, spinach, and shiitake mushroom tart,
      73

    red, and chayote salad, 87

    soup, escarole and, 38

    white, 81

beet soup, roasted, 41

black bean soup, 30

blueberry:

    and balsamic dressing, 65

    purée, pear pudding with, 157

    tart with almond crust, 149

Brazilian okra with cilantro, 80

broccolini and chayote pasta salad, 48

butternut squash soup, 31

cacciatore, chicken, 119

caldo verde, 34

caramelizing, 4

cashew nuts, brown rice with cranberries and, 63

ceviche, 13

chayote:

    and broccolini pasta salad, 48

    and red bean salad, 87

cherry dressing, 60

chicken:

    cacciatore, 119

    in caldo verde, 34

    cups, Thai, 126

    curried stew, 118

    cutlets, 25

    grilled, 122

    mushroom, and zucchini soup, 45

    roast, stuffed with herbed pistachio gremolata,
      114

    roast, with vegetables, 111

    roll-ups, 25

    salad salpicao, 49

    salt-crusted, 115

    and shrimp stew (ximxim), 134-35

    stock, 162

Chinese-style steamed red snapper, 98

cilantro, Brazilian okra with, 80

coconut:

    cookies (doce de coco), 158

    pudding (pudim de coco), 140

coleslaw, 52

collard greens, 69

cookies, coconut (doce de coco), 158

corn soup, 35

covering, 4

crabmeat-stuffed mushrooms, 14

cranberries, brown rice with cashew nuts and, 63

croutons, 43

curried chicken stew, 118

deglazing, 4

desserts:

    arroz doce (rice pudding), 153

    blueberry tart with almond crust, 149

    doce de abobora (pumpkin dessert), 152

    doce de coco (coconut cookies), 158

    egg white flan, 148

    light floating islands, 159

    pear pudding with blueberry purée, 157

doce de abobora (pumpkin dessert), 152

doce de coco (coconut cookies), 158

dried fruits, 6

eggplant:

    in grilled vegetables, 76

    Japanese, 72

    Japanese, in antipasto, 12

    rolled, 142–43

egg white flan, 148

equipment, 8

escarole and bean soup, 38

farofa, 138

fennel, in roasted beet soup, 41

fish:

    ahi poke (tuna with mango salsa), 105

    Chinese-style steamed red snapper, 98

    grilled marinated salmon, 108

    herbed rainbow trout, 99

    "in a bag," 7

    in ceviche, 13

    orange roughy with herbed tomato sauce, 109

    pistachio-crusted sea bass, 104

    salmon in parchment, five ways, 110

    salmon spread roll-ups, 18–19

    seared sea bass, 101

    stock, 163

    tuna spread roll-ups, 20

flan:

    egg white, 148

    pudim de leite, 139

fruits, dried, 6

garlic, roasted, and tofu spread, 21

gazpacho, tomato, 36

grains, 5–6

    brown rice with cashew nuts and cranberries, 63

    quinoa tabbouleh, 64

    rice pilaf, 137

    rice pudding (arroz doce), 153

    wild rice and vegetable salad, 56

    wild rice-stuffed tomatoes, 93

green grape salsa, 15

gremolata, herbed pistachio, for roast chicken, 114

guacamole, 16

Hawaiian steamed salmon, 110

herbs, herbed, 5

    oven-dried tomatoes, 71

    rainbow trout, 99

honey mustard dressing, 50

ingredients, 5–7

Italian steamed salmon, 110

Japanese eggplant, 72
    in antipasto, 12

kale, 69
kelp, in miso soup, 42
knife technique, 4

leftovers, 7
lentil soup, 39
light floating islands, 159

mango salsa, 169
    for ahi poke (tuna), 105
marinades, 6
    for broccolini and chayote pasta salad, 48
    for grilled chicken, 122
    for grilled turkey tenderloins, 123
    for shrimp in big salad, 129
    for vegetables in big salad with shrimp, 128
    for wild rice and vegetable salad, 56
marinated roast turkey, 132
mayonnaise, 168
Mediterranean steamed salmon, 110
miso soup, 42
mushroom(s):
    crabmeat-stuffed, 14
    cremini, in stuffed yellow squash, 89
    garbanzo bean and spinach tart with shiitake, 73
    medley, 78
    zucchini, and chicken soup, 45
mustard greens, 69

nuts, 6
    almond crust, blueberry tart with, 149
    cashew, brown rice with cranberries and, 63
    peanut, tofu, and roasted onion dressing, 51
    pistachio-crusted sea bass, 104
    pistachio gremolata, roast chicken stuffed with, 114

okra:
    Brazilian, with cilantro, 80
    and tomatoes, 79
onions, roasted:
    in peanut and tofu dressing, 51
    in simple salad, 57
orange roughy with herbed tomato sauce,
    109
oriental steamed salmon, 110

pad "not" Thai, 86
papaya dressing, 50
pasta salad with broccolini and chayote,
    48
peanut, tofu, and roasted onion dressing, 51
pea purée, 83
pear pudding with blueberry purée, 157
peppers, roasted, 6
    red, and asparagus, 68
pilaf, 137
pineapple dressing, 65
pistachio:
    -crusted sea bass, 104
    gremolata, roast chicken stuffed with, 114
potato sticks, 171
pudding:
    coconut (pudim de coco), 140
    pear, with blueberry purée, 157
    rice (arroz doe), 153
pudim de coco (coconut pudding), 140
pudim de leite (flan), 139
pumpkin dessert (doce de abobora), 152
purée:
    blueberry, pear pudding with, 157
    pea, 83
    sweet potato, 92

quinoa tabbouleh, 64

rainbow trout, herbed, 99

ratatouille, 90

red snapper, Chinese-style steamed, 98

rice:

brown, with cashew nuts and cranberries, 63

noodles, in pad "not" Thai, 86

pilaf, 137

pudding (arroz doce), 153

wild, and vegetable salad, 56

wild rice-stuffed tomatoes, 93

rice paper wrappers, 27

roast chicken:

stuffed with herbed pistachio gremolata, 114

with vegetables, 111

rolled eggplant, 142-43

roll-ups:

chicken, 25

salmon spread, 18-19

tuna spread, 20

rubbing spices, 6

salad dressings, 7

blueberry and balsamic, 65

cherry, 60

honey mustard, 50

papaya, 50

peanut, tofu, and roasted onion, 51

pineapple, 65

soy-ginger, 60

salads:

big, with shrimp, 128-29

broccolini and chayote pasta, 48

brown rice, with cashew nuts and cranberries, 63

chicken salpicao, 49

coleslaw, 52

quinoa tabbouleh, 64

red bean and chayote, 87

simple, 57

vibrant slaw, 53

salmon:

grilled marinated, 108

-spread roll-ups, 18-19

steamed, 110

salpicao, chicken salad, 49

salsas:

green grape, 15

mango, basic, 169

mango, for ahi poke (tuna), 105

salt-crusted chicken, 115

sauce(s), 4

basic tomato, 166

herbed tomato, for orange roughy, 109

mayonnaise, 168

plum, for Thai chicken cups, 126

scampi, for seared scallops, 102

for seared sea bass, 101

for ximxim (chicken and shrimp stew), 135

sautéing, 4

scallops with scampi sauce, 102

sea bass:

pistachio-crusted, 104

seared, 101

seared sea bass, 101

seeds, 6

shellfish:

in ceviche, 13

crabmeat-stuffed mushrooms, 14

seared scallops with scampi sauce, 102

shrimp:

big salad with, 128-29

and chicken stew (ximxim), 134-35

simple salad, 57

soups:

black bean, 30

butternut squash, 31

caldo verde, 34

corn, 35

escarole and bean, 38

lentil, 39

miso, 42

roasted beet, 41

tomato gazpacho, 36

zucchini, chicken, and mushroom, 45

soy-ginger dressing, 60

spaghetti, vegetable, 95

spaghetti squash with tomato sauce, 88

spices, rubbing, 6

spinach, in garbanzo bean and shiitake mushroom

tart, 73

spreads:

roasted garlic and tofu, 21

salmon, 19

tuna, 20

spring rolls, 27

squash:

butternut soup, 31

spaghetti, with tomato sauce, 88

stuffed yellow, 89

in vegetable spaghetti, 95

steamed red snapper, Chinese-style,

98

steaming in parchment, 110

stews:

curried chicken, 118

vegetable, 90

ximxim (chicken and shrimp), 134–35

stocks, 4

chicken, 162

fish, 163

vegetable, 167

stuffed cherry tomatoes, 19

stuffed yellow squash, 89

sweet potato purée, 92

tabbouleh, quinoa, 64

tart:

blueberry, with almond crust, 149

garbanzo bean, spinach, and shiitake mushroom, 73

techniques, 4

Thai chicken cups, 126

Thai steamed salmon, 110

tofu:

in miso soup, 42

peanut and roasted onion dressing with,

51

spread, roasted garlic and, 21

tomato(es):

in antipasto, 12

gazpacho, 36

herbed oven-dried, 71

okra and, 79

sauce, basic, 166

sauce for spaghetti squash, 88

stuffed, 19

wild rice-stuffed, 93

trout, herbed rainbow, 99

tuna:

with mango salsa (ahi poke), 105

spread roll-ups, 20

turkey:

grilled tenderloins, 123

marinated roast, 132

vegetable(s), 68–95

grilled, 6, 76

roast chicken and, 111

spaghetti, 95

stew, 90

stock, 167

wild rice salad and, 56

see also specific vegetables

vibrant slaw salad, 53

weekend recipes, 126–43
    big salad with shrimp, 128–29
    farofa, 138
    marinated roast turkey, 132
    pudim de coco (coconut pudding), 140
    pudim de leite (flan), 139
    rice pilaf, 137
    rolled eggplant, 142–43
    Thai chicken cups, 126
    ximxim (chicken and shrimp stew), 134–35
white beans, 81

wild rice:
    -stuffed tomatoes, 93
    and vegetable salad, 56
wonton skins, Thai chicken cups in, 126

ximxim (chicken and shrimp stew),
    134–35

yucca, 138

zucchini, chicken, and mushroom soup, 45